Make Your
Moments
Count

Victorious Living Collection
30 Day Devotional

Sarah Malanowski and Friends

Scripture quotations marked (AMP) are taken from the *Amplified Bible*, Copyright © 1954, 1958, 1962, 1964, 1965, 1987 by The Lockman Foundation. Used by permission.

Scripture quotations marked (ESV) are from The Holy Bible, *English Standard Version*, Copyright © 2001 by Crossway Bibles, a publishing ministry of Good News Publishers. Used by permission. All rights reserved.

Scripture marked (GW) is taken from *GOD'S WORD*. Copyright © 1995 God's Word to the Nations. Used by permission of Baker Publishing Group. All rights reserved.

Scripture quotations marked (MSG) are taken from *The Message*. Copyright © 1993, 1994, 1995, 1996, 2000, 2001, 2002. Used by permission of NavPress Publishing Group.

Scripture quotations marked (NASB) are taken from the *New American Standard Bible*, Copyright © 1960, 1962, 1963, 1968, 1971, 1972, 1973, 1975, 1977, 1995 by The Lockman Foundation. Used by permission.

Scripture quotations marked (NKJV) are taken from the *New King James Version*. Copyright © 1982 by Thomas Nelson, Inc. Used by permission. All rights reserved.

Scripture quotations marked (NLT) are taken from the Holy Bible, *New Living Translation*, copyright © 1996. Used by permission of Tyndale House Publishers, Inc., Wheaton, Illinois 60189. All rights reserved.

Scripture quotations marked (RSV) are from *Revised Standard Version of the Bible*, copyright © 1946, 1952, and 1971 National Council of the Churches of Christ in the United States of America. Used by permission. All rights reserved.

Scripture quotations marked (TLB) are taken from *The Living Bible* / Kenneth N. Taylor: Tyndale House, © Copyright 1997, 1971 by Tyndale House Publishers, Inc. Used by permission. All rights reserved.

Scripture quotations marked (NIV) are taken from the Holy Bible, *New International Version*, niv. Copyright © 1973, 1978, 1984 by Biblica, Inc.™ Used by permission of Zondervan. All rights reserved worldwide. www.zondervan.com.

Printed in United States of America

ISBN: 978-1-947066-00-7
1. Family & Relationships/Parenting/Motherhood
2. Religion/Christian Life/Inspirational

Cover & Book Design by Sondra Howe
Scripture Art by Krystal Whitten, Jessica Serrano, Karissa Birberick, Isabella Moore and Shutterstock.

What Others Are Saying

"With practical tips and life lessons for moms in every stage of life, readers will learn to cling to hope in the face of despair, triumph over tragedies, and learn the biggest lesson of them all—that they are not alone."

— Michelle S. Lazurek
Award-Winning Author
Pastor's Wife and Speaker

"When a baby is born, we marvel at the miracle of birth—and well, we should. Yet it is no less of a miracle that in that same instant, God creates within the soul of the woman a mother's heart. In this book, Sarah has put the miracle of a mother's heart for her children on full display. As you read this collection of daily devotionals, you will find a unity of spirit and a diversity of ideas while also experiencing the passion and patience as well as the wit and warmth of mothers from every stage of life. In these pages, a woman will find encouragement, companionship, courage, and hope. The hard part will be waiting until tomorrow to hear the next heart."

— Glen Howe
Associate Pastor of Discipleship
First Baptist Church Jonesboro, Georgia

"In **Make Your Moments Count**, Sarah Malanowski and friends were able to powerfully and affectionately communicate the life lessons that I wholeheartedly desire for my children—Robbie, Tyler, and Keira. May they always remember His unconditional love and endless grace for them."

— Sandy Rinchuse
Manager of Preschool Ministries
Exciting Idlewild Baptist Church, Tampa, Florida

"I heartily recommend starting your day by reading **Make Your Moments Count**. The Godly wisdom and insights of Sarah Malanowski and her friends could easily fill volumes. Prayerfully chosen selections have been included in this mighty devotional book providing a delicious dose of extravagant blessings to nourish moms each day."

— Jo Ann Custer
Director of Preschool Ministries
Exciting Idlewild Baptist Church, Tampa, Florida

"For the last five months, we have begun each day with one of the thirty-day devotional readings by Sarah Malanowski. After breakfast, finishing the last cup of coffee, Alice reads to me Sarah's practical, simply profound insight into a biblical truth—to begin our day setting our minds on things above and committing our day to the Lord.

The scope of this new thirty-day devotional is expanded by the insights of twenty loving, devoted moms—each seeking to instill into her children deep, penetrating, and sometimes painful truth, such as consider it pure joy and in everything, give thanks! Sarah finishes 'the month' with the top ten lessons she and Paul want Zion and Gabriel to build into their lives before they leave home.

No matter your age, each narrative is a thought-provoking way to begin your day—setting your eyes on Jesus, the Author and Perfecter of our faith!

Dear Lord Jesus, thank You for the wonderful insights You are giving to these precious mothers who are leading their children to walk daily in Your presence."

— David A. Pletincks
Pastor
Hope Community Bible Church, Spring Hill, Florida

"Have you ever heard the saying 'I wish children came with a manual'? As believers, our guidebook for anything in life comes straight from the Bible. However, the words of wisdom included in this book that Sarah has compiled from other mothers are an amazing addition to the Word of God. I love hearing their hearts through the written Word and knowing that they have walked paths that I have walked and will soon walk. I highly recommend this book for mothers, grandmothers, and soon-to-be mamas."

— Courtney Chesney
Minister's Wife
Homeschool Mom of Four

Make Your Moments Count is a thought-provoking insightful aid for parents and grandparents in their quest to instill godly principles and characteristics in their children from Scripture.

Each 'life lesson' offers a practical, attainable goal that both encourages and inspires the reader to walk in God's presence.

Sarah has a pure heart and genuine desire to glorify God in every aspect of her life. This spills over to her commitment to raise her own children according to God's plan, thus the out-growth being the creation of ***Make Your Moments Count***.

As a mother of four adult children, I would have loved to have had this resource while raising them but look forward to implementing these principles and influencing my grandchildren."

— Kim Griffin
Minister's wife
Married 34 years
Four children, 5 grandchildren

Dedicated to

Our brave and beautiful children, may your eyes forever be fixed on Jesus, the Author and Perfecter of your faith!

Nate, Levi, and Gabe, you are so amazing! Dad and I are proud and humbled as we watch you parent your young children with tenderness and strength in God's truth.

I love you so much, Mom/Ma/Mama

. . . . .

Isaac, Libby, Sam, Luke, and Joel—you are treasures to me and Dad from our Almighty God, and we cherish each of you! My heart's desire is that you walk with Him all your days and seek Him first in all things. Be straight shooters, my arrows!

Love, Mom

. . . . .

Just the thought of you all makes my heart leap. Adriana, Aria, and Atlas, I've been given visions of greatness for each of your lives. May God's words breathe life into these pages and into your hearts.

Love you forever, Mom

. . . . .

Caleb, you are a gift from God. Dad and I are blessed daily as we watch you grow in Christ and serve Him. Continue to be bold and courageous for Him! Mwen renmen ou!

Mom

To the ones who create such joy on this roller-coaster ride called life—Dominic, Isabella, Eleanora, Zander, Annalina, Garrison, and Christiana. Thank you for helping me put my hands in the air and enjoy it!

Love you! Mommy

. . . . .

Isaiah—our joyful, miracle boy! Daddy and I consider it a great honor to be your parents! You have always smiled your way through life despite all of the trials you've endured. Jesus will continue to give you contagious joy and strength as you live for Him.

With love, Mommy

. . . . .

Micaiah, Elias, Toby, and Naamiah—no words will ever convey how proud we are of you and how blessed I am to be your mom. I will always pray Colossians 1:9–12 over you and your future families!

Love, Mom

. . . . .

Harper, Paisley, and Skyler, words will never come close in capturing my love for you. I am blessed every day that I am able to call myself your mother. The Lord has blessed me abundantly, and you are my greatest treasure. I will never stop believing in you, encouraging you, and loving you. I am never far.

Love, Mom

. . . . .

Jake, Isaac, Eli, Aliyah, and Saylah—thank you for making me a mom, you have taught me so much. I love each of you dearly and delight in your unique personalities! Keep growing into who God created you to be, and keep your eyes on Him. You are my favorites!

Love, Mom

Eli, Toby, Ish, and Julian—Dad and I are forever in your corners, rooting on God's best for your lives. You are so very loved.

Mom, 1 Timothy 4:9–12

. . . . .

Grant and Sydney, Dad and I are so proud of you both, and love watching you step into all God has for you. Love God, love people, and dream big.

Love, Mom and Dad

. . . . .

Abigail, Lydia, and Joel, we have been through a lot this year, but God has continued to be faithful, hasn't He! I am so blessed to be called your mama. I love you all!

Love, Mom

. . . . .

Grant and Lexi, my heart is so full with love and joy that God has granted my heart's desire of being your mommy. If you remember one thing, and one thing only, never forget that God loves you more than anyone—so much that He gave His Son Jesus to save you—and true life can be found only through faith in Christ Jesus. There is no greater advice I could ever give you.

Love, Mommy

. . . . .

Christi and Curtis: As you begin the journey through your twenties, I am increasingly aware that my time of "actively parenting" you is coming to an end. I hope and pray that you have God's Word deeply planted in the roots of your heart and soul. I pray that it is His voice that you hear in your spirit when you are faced with a choice. And as you go, may you let your light shine in a way that brings glory to God.

Love, Mom

Claire, Joel, and Grace—your dad and I have been extremely blessed with the three of you! You are amazing gifts from God. I am forever thankful to be your mom. I pray you walk closely with the Lord throughout this life.

I love you so much, Momma

. . . . .

Pierce and Haven, you two are my treasures. I am so proud and blessed to be your mom. Your dad and I love you and pray that the Lord will capture your hearts at an early age and you will live for Him. Be strong and courageous.

Love, Mom

. . . . .

Kelly, Karis, Karly, Josh, Megan, Brice, Bella, and Ashton—Dad and I are so proud of who you are and who you are becoming! You bring us great joy! We pray you will always be able to discern what is best (Phil.1:10) and choose to follow Jesus with all your heart.

Love always, Mom (Nana)

. . . . .

Cade, Claire, Caris, and Corrie—may you continue to be the salt of the earth and a light in this world for Christ. Your dad and I are beyond proud to be your parents, and we look forward to seeing all God has in store for your future. Shine bright and dream big.

Love, Mom

. . . . .

Ellie, Saedi, Isaac, Solomon, Josiah, Gideon, and Gabe—you are my favorite treasures! Our tears and laughter have made me the richest momma. You will never lose your worth—which is more than gold! Walk with God, be kind, and do the right thing.

Love, Momma

Thomas, Maggie, Scoty, Georgia, and Charlie—one of the greatest pleasures of my life has been being your mama, watching you grow into the people you are becoming. Thank you for the joy and laughter. Keep laughing, keep loving people, and keep your eyes fixed on Jesus. I love you from the depth of my heart and soul.

Love, Mama

. . . . .

Zion and Gabriel, my strong and brave warriors, I pray that you will live valiant lives for Christ. May you learn early on what it means to *Make Your Moments Count*! I love you both so much, and I'm extremely proud to have you as my sons.

Love, Mom

O Israel, listen: Jehovah is our God, Jehovah alone. You must love him with all your heart, soul, and might. And you must think constantly about these commandments I am giving you today. **You must teach them to your children and talk about them when you are at home or out for a walk;** *at bedtime and the first thing in the morning. Tie them on your finger, wear them on your forehead, and write them on the doorposts of your house!*

— Deuteronomy 6:4–9 (TLB)

Contents

About the Author 15

Foreword 21

Introduction 23

Day 1: Christ Is Enough 27

Day 2: Fear Not 31

Day 3: Love First 35

Day 4: I Love This Moment 39

Day 5: Conformer Versus Transformer 43

Day 6: Speak Life 47

Day 7: Stay Focused 51

Day 8: Cultivate a Listening Ear 55

Day 9: Expect Troubles 59

Day 10: The Hero's Secret 63

Day 11: By Faith (Insert Your Name Here) 67

Day 12: Standing Firm 71

Day 13: Rejoice in the Lord Always 75

Day 14: Be You 79

Day 15: Your Generation 83

Day 16: Grace 87

Day 17: The Best Is Yet to Come 91

Day 18: Hard Pressed on Every Side 95

Day 19: Brave Children Hold God's Hand 99

Day 20: Hide and Seek 103

Day 21: Make the Most of Every Opportunity 107

Day 22: Become a Grace Dispenser 109

Day 23: The Art of Listening 111

Day 24: Walk Tall and Stand Strong 113

Day 25: There is Always Room for Growth 115

Day 26: Obedience Is the Key 117

Day 27: Keep in Step with the Lord 119

Day 28: Only Speak What Edifies 121

Day 29: Remember Who You Are 123

Day 30: Appreciate the Gift Giver 125

Bibliography 128

Contents

About the author
Foreword
Introduction
Day 1:
Day 2:
Day 3:
Day 4:
Day 5:
Day 6:
Day 7:
Day 8:
Day 9:
Day 10:
Day 11:
Day 12:
Day 13:
Day 14:
Day 15:
Day 16:
Day 17:
Day 18:
Day 19:
Day 20:
Day 21:
Day 22:
Day 23:
Day 24:
Day 25:
Day 26:
Day 27:
Day 28:
Day 29:
Day 30:
Bibliography

About the Author

To enjoy more devotionals by Sarah, you can go to her website:
Godisalwaysfaithful.com

Optimizing Lives for Eternal Impact

Also, find Sarah at:

Facebook: https://www.facebook.com/godisalwaysfaithful7
Twitter: @sarahmalanowski
Pinterest: God is Always Faithful.

You can also enjoy more books in the *Victorious Living Collection*:

Joyful Living
Praying through the Gospels
Victorious Mindset
Wisdom for Life
Clinging to God's Promises

More books to come in the *Victorious Living Collection* soon!

Other books by Sarah:

Life's Compass for Eternal Treasure
His Hope for your Destiny

Victorious Living Collection

Joyful Living

Sarah Malanowski
(Sarah Beth Lindberg)

Do the storms of life have you discouraged? Have you lost your joy? Do you need a reminder that God is still faithful? If you answered yes to any of these questions, then *Joyful Living* is the book for you.

The abundant life in Christ begins with a state of joy. Joy is a choice that you can make every day. You do not have to be weighed down by the burdens of your storm. God is on the throne, and He wants you to know He will be faithful through this. Nothing is too big for God! Take up the joy of Jesus daily and find rest for your soul in *Joyful Living*.

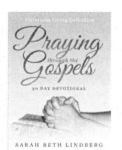

Praying through the Gospels

Sarah Malanowski
(Sarah Beth Lindberg)

A recent study by the Barna Group indicated that more than 90% of Christians desire a closer relationship with God. Are you among this majority?

A closer relationship with God starts with a better understanding of His Son, Jesus Christ. In *Praying through the Gospels*, you will encounter the sweet moments of Jesus' life and learn how to apply His wisdom to your life. These prayers will guide you and teach you how to walk more faithfully with the Lord.

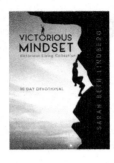

Victorious Mindset

Sarah Malanowski
(Sarah Beth Lindberg)

Victorious Mindset is a book designed to help you overcome the battles that take place in your mind. In thirty days, you can change how you think. You can learn to use your mind for the work of God and become a force to be reckoned with. So let's get off the devil's playground and start using our minds to serve Jesus.

Wisdom for Life

Sarah Malanowski
(Sarah Beth Lindberg)

Billy Graham once said, "Knowledge is horizontal. Wisdom is vertical—it comes down from above." Wisdom from God is free, and you can have as much of it as you desire. In fact, that's exactly what God says in James 1:5: "If any of you lacks wisdom, he should ask God, who gives generously to all without finding fault, and it will be given to him."

God's wisdom can empower you to live a life that matters. Wisdom for Life invites you to take a journey through the Proverbs to discover the wisdom God has for you. May the words that Solomon penned become your guide, and may God's Spirit increase your spiritual stature in wisdom as you read through this thirty-day devotional.

Clinging to God's Promises

Sarah Malanowski
(Sarah Beth Lindberg)

God works all things together for your good. He promises that He will never leave you or forsake you. He who began a good work in you will be faithful to complete it. Absolutely nothing can separate you from the love of God. These are just a few of the verses that you will find in this book.

There is a treasure trove of beauty offered in the pages of this book as you daily discover the promises God has for you as His child. Each promise will remind you that you are God's prized creation. He knows you, He loves you, and He has called you by name.

You were meant to live a victorious life in Christ. Come experience this victory as you cling to and embrace over a hundred verses in God's Word that were written just for you.

Foreword

All of us would agree the Word of God is our greatest source of wisdom that gives us truth and instruction for life. Sometimes along with the Word, we need encouragement from an earthly vessel who is living out her own salvation with fear and trembling, as she balances her family life with her spiritual life.

The book you hold in your hand is filled with the wisdom as well as stories and challenges of "fellow moms" who will not only make you feel "normal" but will highlight examples of mothers of all ages covered in grace. Sometimes we are so close to our routines of life, we need a fresh look from above, along with life lessons from below.

Thank you, Sarah and comrade moms, for thirty days of devotions that help us to lighten our load and remind each of us that the blessing of being a mom is not just a privilege, but a high calling from Almighty God. In that calling, we are not only allowed to laugh at our mistakes but learn from our journey and share our joys and defeats. The lives of these moms will cheer you on to do what you do best—being a mom to the glory of God.

— Ginny Whitten
Married 40 years, 4 children, and 11 grandchildren
Pastor's wife at Exciting Idlewild Baptist Church in Tampa, Florida

Introduction

Motherhood. That beautiful yet crazy, sweet yet sometimes sour, fun yet hard, exciting yet scary, thrilling and yet exhausting time of life that I'm still learning how to appreciate and enjoy! It can be tough to navigate what is most important to teach my sons before they leave home. Of course, the ultimate goal is to cultivate their hearts for the Lord. But what else is essential for them to know before they leave our home?

The pursuit of identifying the top ten life lessons to give my children has been a sweet one. My husband and I embarked on this journey about two years ago, shortly after a conversation with a friend who shared their family mottos with us. It was one of those aha moments when we walked away saying, "Let's do that for our family."

We started writing them down and soon realized how nice it would be to have them in a book. However, ten mottos meant only ten devotionals for a thirty-devotional book. It was then that God put on my heart to invite twenty other moms to join me in the adventure of writing a book. This was perfect, as one of our family mottos is to never stop learning. We want our boys to remain teachable through life gleaning from the wisdom of those around them.

Hence, the perfect fit of twenty moms and myself presenting the top lessons we want our children to learn before leaving home. These lessons have been written by women I admire, women who love Jesus, women who are serving the King, and women who are doing their best to make the moments count in their homes. Some of these women have mentored me through childhood, college, and adulthood. Some have shared in the struggles of life with me. Others have been walking with me hand in hand through this crazy adventure of parenthood. It's a tremendous honor and blessing to give you this next book in the

Victorious Living Collection from twenty friends and myself. I pray that as you read it, you will receive fresh perspective for the journey, joy in the mundane tasks, and abundant grace for the moments ahead. Come embark on this expedition with us as we embrace what it means to *Make Your Moments Count*.

In each devotional you will see a shell or starfish above the quote. Please use this as a point of reference to stop and reflect on the wisdom that day's reading provides. Also, included in every devotional is a prayer. May this be a prayer that you and your children can pray together as you reflect on all that God is and wants to be for you.

Throughout the book you will find various Scripture Art from moms and one young lady Isabella. It is our hope and prayer that you will use these to meditate on God's goodness and reflect on who He is for your home. Several of these will be available on my website at https://godisalwaysfaithful.com/resources/ where you can print them off and use them in your home.

I pray that each devotional will be a breath of fresh air to you and that you will be infused with hope and strength for the trek ahead, as you read them.

Embracing Motherhood with You,
Sarah

LOVE THE LORD your GOD WITH all YOUR HEART WITH all YOUR SOUL AND WITH all YOUR MIGHT

Deuteronomy 6:5

k.whitten

Day 1 is lovingly contributed by Krystal Whitten, who is a stay-at-home "mompreneur" of two children, ages five and three. She is a graphic designer and hand-letterer who uses her creative gifts to "letter for the Lord" and encourage women to learn and to delight in God's Word. She enjoys reading, coffee chats, and binge-watching shows on Netflix with her husband once the kids are in bed. You can learn more about Krystal by going to her website, http://krystalwhitten.com.

Day 1

CHRIST IS ENOUGH

For he satisfies the longing soul, and the hungry soul he fills with good things.

— Psalm 107:9 (ESV)

Life Lesson: Only He Can Satisfy

My son is five, and like most children, he lives in the moment. Each day, when I pick him up from preschool, I can expect one of these questions: "Can we go to McDonald's?" "Can we get a slushy?" "Can I go to my cousin's house?" "Can we go to Target and get a toy?" He's been thinking about this specific thing, whatever it is, and he's convinced in that moment that if I would just say yes to one of these questions, it will make him happy. Forever.

This frustrates me because, obviously, I know that no Happy Meal/drink/playtime/toy is going to keep him happy for the rest of his life, always and forever, amen. It'll make him happy in the moment…until the next time.

Not too long ago, it hit me. I wonder if God looks at me and says, "You do the same thing." Because so many times I pray that if God would just answer this one prayer, give me this one thing I want, I will be good to go. Thank you, Lord. I've got it from here. That is, until the next crisis arises or I get a burning desire for something else.

Life promises us a lot of things and delivers none of the lasting satisfaction we expect. I'm thirty-three years old, and I'm really just beginning to understand that. That couch that I just had to have a few years ago has never been comfortable to sit on, and I'd love to get a new one now. That car crisis that we prayed about and God provided funds for isn't the last car crisis we're going to have. Whether it's a need or a want, the never-ending thirst for more follows us through life, doesn't it? If we continue to expect the "more" to satisfy, we'll eventually be discouraged and disillusioned.

Because the truth is, there will always be something new and exciting that promises fulfillment. You're looking to your family, your work, your money, your volunteer commitments, your friends, whatever it is—and you're expecting them to keep you satisfied. The trouble is, none of those things has the power to satisfy you.

Jesus addressed this truth with the Samaritan woman at the well: "Jesus answered, 'Everyone who drinks this water will be thirsty again, but whoever drinks the water I give them will never thirst. Indeed, the water I give them will become in them a spring of water welling up to eternal life'" (John 4:13–14).

As you grow, my children, I want to teach you that nothing, nothing— not even ministry work and serving others—can substitute for faithfully walking with Christ, having a consistent daily time with Him in His Word and in prayer. Because He fills every need of our hearts. Because He is the ultimate good thing.

I love David's prayer in Psalm 16:11: "In your *presence* there is fullness of joy; at your right hand are pleasures forevermore" (ESV, *emphasis mine*).

When you are filled with His presence, you have the energy to live out your callings more effectively without being drained by the people and demands in your lives. When you're satisfied in the Lord, your hearts are tuned to the needs of others rather than run down and overwhelmed with what you want or don't have.

LORD, Your presence is truly all that I need. Just as David said in Psalm 16:2, "You are my Lord; I have no good apart from you," so I desire to live with that same attitude and mind-set. Help me to be intentional to live not entangled with the world but fully abiding in You.

"God and God alone is man's highest good. God is the Creator and sustainer of all things, the source of all being and of all life, and the abundant fountain of all goods."
— Herman Bavinck

Day 2 is lovingly contributed by Paula Davis, who is a wife of seventeen years to full-time seminary student Jonathan Davis and a full-time mom to Abigail (thirteen), Lydia (eleven), and her cancer warrior Joel, who is ten. She enjoys working from home, caring for her family, reading, and occasionally, she can be found inspiring women on her blog at www.AverageHousewife.com.

Day 2
FEAR NOT

Fear not, for I am with you; be not dismayed, for I am your God; I will strengthen you, I will help you, I will uphold you with my righteous right hand.

— Isaiah 41:10 (ESV)

⟩ Life Lesson: When God Is with You, You Have Nothing to Fear ⟨

The times I have struggled most with fear in my life are when I'm in a waiting period and the future is unknown. One of the biggest lessons that God has taught me is that I have nothing to fear. The reason you and I have nothing to fear is because we serve the one and only God. He is great and powerful! He created everything that we see—the earth around us, the galaxies beyond our night stars, and even the cells that make up our body.

Not only is God our Creator, but He is sovereign over all of His creation. He didn't just leave us to figure out life, but He has a plan for each one of us, and He promises that all things work together for our good! God is always faithful and trustworthy. Even though what you experience might not be at all what you had planned, God is not surprised. He will be with you through each step, one at a time.

For I, the Lord your God, hold your right hand; it is I who say to you, "Fear not, I am the one who helps you."

(Isaiah 41:13, ESV)

May you take steps on the path that God has for you without fear. May you remember that God is always with you and He will be your strength and hope. May you remember that He works all things for good for those who love Him.

DEAR GOD, my Creator, there is none like You! I pray that I would not fear but that I would remember that You are with me. You hold my right hand and help me. May I remember these truths when the world and even my own thoughts try to convince me differently. May I walk with the strength that You give, knowing that all my hope is in You, my faithful and trustworthy God.

"Every time fear freezes and worry writhes, every time I surrender to stress, aren't I advertising the unreliability of God? That I really don't believe? But if I'm grateful to the Bridge Builder for the crossing of a million strong bridges, thankful for a million faithful moments, my life speaks my beliefs and I trust Him again. I fearlessly cross the next bridge. I shake my head at the blinding wonder of it: Trust is the bridge from yesterday to tomorrow, built with planks of thanks. Remembering frames up gratitude. Gratitude lays out the planks of trust. I can walk the planks—from known to unknown—and know: He holds. I could walk unafraid."

— Ann Voskamp

Mightier THAN THE waves OF · THE · SEA · is His love for you

PSALM 93:4

Day 3 is lovingly contributed by Stephanie Conklin, who is a wife to pastor-husband, Mark, and mom to four forces-to-be-reckoned-with sons. Steph gets most excited when she and her family can be involved in meeting others' needs—from those desperate for physical provision to those materially comfortable yet missing out on the abundant life of Jesus. Despite years of practice, Steph remains the only one in her household who cannot spiral a football.

Day 3
LOVE FIRST

We love because he first loved us. — 1 John 4:19

> **Life Lesson: Love with the Love You Have Been Given**

I hope as you strike out on your own, you'll remember the things we've walked through together. "Hold the door for the people behind you." "Give sacrificially of yourself and your possessions." "Choose not to complain but instead to be a part of the solution." Yet truly, so many of the lessons that I want to make sure you take with you can boil down to two words: **love first**.

- Before you take offense at the way someone responds to you, **love first**.
- Before you judge someone's actions, **love first**.
- Before you think you can do it better than them, **love first**.
- Before you think you are too busy to help, **love first**.
- Before you feel an authority figure does not deserve your submission, **love first**.

It is only when we **love first** that we are then in the right place to move forward. We cannot diffuse a situation if we are coming in armed with our own self-righteousness. We cannot understand a person's motives without genuinely caring for him. We cannot offer grace if we think it has to be earned.

It seems so simple, but choosing to **love first** is a challenge every moment of every day. It is putting self second, giving the benefit of the doubt, passing out a million chances. It is heart over brain, countercultural, not always black and white. It can hurt.

Yet it is how God loves us. He looks past our surface and to our heart, passes over our pride and ignorance, gives us more chances than can be counted, and keeps loving us no matter how we respond. He starts with love, and through Him, we can too. Love first.

This is love: not that we loved God, but that he loved us and sent his Son as an atoning sacrifice for our sins. Dear friends, since God so loved us, we also ought to love one another. No one has ever seen God; but if we love one another, God lives in us and his love is made complete in us.

(1 John 4:10–12)

FATHER, I cannot grasp the depths of Your unconditional love and boundless mercy. Thank You for loving me before my heart was even turned toward You, for choosing me though I had nothing You needed. Forgive me for the many times I do not reflect Your love in how I treat others. May Your Holy Spirit love through me. Amen.

"Intense love does not measure, it just gives."

— Mother Teresa

For HE WILL ORDER HIS angels to Protect you WHEREVER you go

psalm 91:11

Day 4 is lovingly contributed by Melinda Nelson, who is a wife and teammate to a handyman. She is mother to five kids who help her live in the now. She is a writer, reader, coffee drinker, homeschooler, dabbler in many venues, eclectic creator who sees beauty in junk and whose favorite color is patina rust. She can be found sharing her creative side at https://restoredfacets.wordpress.com/.

Day 4

I LOVE THIS MOMENT

This is the day that the LORD has made; let us rejoice and be glad in it.

— Psalm 118:24 (ESV)

Life Lesson: Embrace the Ordinary

The thought washed over me as I sat wedged between my two preteen girls, all cuddled in and warm. Our family was watching some random Netflix show, probably about food—it didn't matter—it was a fairly common scenario. The day had been just a normal day, the ones the majority of our family life consists of: school, chores, housework, meals, avoiding the chilly winter outdoors if possible. Nothing huge had happened, no big mom wins, no insightful conversations or amazing feats of strength or mind. It was a day that many would describe as ordinary, one of those days that make up the framework of one's life—stable and doused in routine but nothing that stands out, nothing that will be remembered for years to come.

Yet it was a good day. A lovely day.

That moment cocooned with my girls as my boys and men sat around us chilling in silence was gold. It was comfort. It was a lull in the busy of life. It was a cozy place to land. It was home.

Not every moment will be extraordinary. In fact, the vast majority of them will be simple, unassuming, and quiet—ordinary. Try not to spend your life focused on the next thrill, the next amazing planned-out moment. Experience the now. The sometimes ordinary but always a divine miracle of right now.

Finding gratefulness and contentment in your ordinary will not only enhance your days, it will encourage your mind to stand in awe of the little things, and it will open your eyes to the world around you. To God all around you. Embracing ordinary brings new dimension to your life, your world, your God. Seeing him in everything brings Him glory and you more depth in your relationship with Him.

Each day is a gift God has given you. No matter how mundane it may be, you are alive, your heart beats its solid rhythm, and your lungs pull the oxygen from the air. It is a good day. He has given you everything you need for this day, and He will not leave your side. Wasting the ordinary days in the pursuit of the next big thing only brushes past the vast majority of your time here on earth. And often, those big things don't turn out to be as big or as amazing as you thought they would be. So wake up each morning thankful that you are here and anticipating that God has beautiful things in store for you that day. Maybe then you will begin to see all those daily gifts an ordinary day can bring.

> *My frame was not hidden from you when I was made in the secret place, when I was woven together in the depths of the earth. Your eyes saw my unformed body; all the days ordained for me were written in your book before one of them came to be.* (Psalm 139:15–16)

JESUS, please open our eyes to the extraordinary around us. May we pause and breathe in the moments that make up our seemingly ordinary days. May we be grateful for all the beauty and grace You have brought into our day. May our hearts rejoice in Your gift of the here and now. Thank You. Amen.

"The only difference between an extraordinary life and an ordinary one is the extraordinary pleasures you find in ordinary things."

— Veronique Vienne

Day 5 is lovingly contributed by Kristina Toman, who is a daughter of the King, wife of Bret, and mom of Isaac, Libby, Sam, Luke, and Joel. She enjoys homeschooling her children, spending time with family, crafting with friends, and drinking coffee with iron-sharpening-iron sisters. She is passionate about helping others discover their spiritual giftedness and about discipleship.

Day 5

CONFORMER VERSES TRANSFORMER

Do not conform to the pattern of this world, but be transformed by the renewing of your mind. Then you will be able to test and approve what God's will is—His good, pleasing and perfect will.

— Romans 12:2

Life Lesson: A Pattern for Your Life

My child, before you were even hoped for by Dad and me, God already knew your timeline. And your timeline is ordained by Him for His purposes. He put you on this earth, at this place in history, knowing the culture and ways of this world in this age. And while He put you here for such a time as this, His desire for you is to be set apart from the world. Culture screams for tolerance and freedom of choice and promotion of self, but God's Holy Word states that we renew our minds, choosing to be set apart.

The Bible tells us not to conform to the pattern of this world. This is what the pattern of this world looks like:

- Addiction to technology
- Use of flippant, disrespectful phrases
- Desire for more stuff and other people's stuff
- Striving for status—best student, best athlete, best musician, etc.

The list goes on, as you well know. But you don't need to follow that pattern. You can choose (and are called to choose) God's design for your life. Making that choice means you do the following:

- *Choose for yourselves this day whom you will serve* (Joshua 24:15).
- *Set an example for the believers in speech, in conduct, in love, in faith, and in purity* (1 Timothy 4:12).
- *Love the Lord your God, and love your neighbor as yourself* (Matthew 22:37–39).
- *Set your minds on things above, not on earthly things* (Colossians 3:2).

As you make these choices, you can be a transformer rather than a conformer. You can be used by God to accomplish His will in this culture and timeline He has chosen for you. Be confident in this, my child. As others see a difference in you and your choices, you will bring Him glory, and that is the point of it all!

Precious Father, strengthen me with the passion and courage to live a life set apart from this culture and prepared to do Your will. Create in me the desire to be a transformer. Fill me with all joy and peace as I trust in You so that I may overflow with hope by the power of the Holy Spirit (Romans 15:13).

"The point of your life is to point to Him. Whatever you are doing, God wants to be glorified, because this whole thing is His."
— Francis Chan

Be careful FOR NOTHING but IN EVERY THING by prayer and supplication WITH THANKSGIVING LET YOUR REQUESTS be made known UNTO G·O·D

Philippians 4:6

Day 6 is lovingly contributed by Joyce Kelly, who is a Bible teacher with a calling and passion to teach God's Word to girls and women. She has been transformed by the power of the Word and has an unstoppable passion to bring others to the knowledge that they too can study the Bible and it can transform their lives! She was the teaching director of Community Bible Study for six years when God called her to her present position of area director, where she oversees three area classes.

God awakened her heart to human trafficking over nine years ago, and through a series of events, God led her to go to some of the darkest places in the Tampa Bay Area. She is the founder of IAMFreedomGirl Ministries. This is a ministry for women in the sex industry. She, along with her team, visits local strip clubs to meet women right where they are to bring the love of Christ. For more information, visit IAMFreedomgirl.com.

She has been married to her husband, Ronn, for 25 years and is blessed by her 18-year-old twins, Grant and Sydney.

Day 6
SPEAK LIFE

The tongue can bring death or life; those who love to talk will reap the consequences.

— Proverbs 18:21 (NLT)

>Life Lesson: Words Matter, Choose Them Wisely!<

This is a lesson that I pray you will take seriously: the significance of your words. In the beginning, God spoke the world into existence! God has established that there is power in our words, so I pray that you would choose them with great care. My prayer is that life-giving words would shape who you are and what you speak about others. That you will be known as a person who speaks grace. You won't always get this right; no one does. Ask for forgiveness and move forward.

Speak life over yourself. This is a lesson that took me a while to learn. It is my prayer that you would learn early of who you are in Christ and that you would live in those truths. Life can be hard, people can be hard, and it's so easy to believe lies about yourself. Doubt, fear, and the uncertainty of life can try and shape who you will become, but I am praying that you will allow the truth of what Jesus says about you to be louder than any other voice.

Speak life over others. This is one of the greatest gifts we can give to others. I pray that you will always see the best in others, even when it's really hard to do so. Before you speak, I pray that you would THINK:

T: Is it true?
H: Is it helpful?
I: Is it inspiring?
N: Is it necessary?
K: Is it kind?

May you use this filter as you choose to speak life into others.

> *Do not let any unwholesome talk come out of your mouths,*
> *but only what is helpful for building others up according to*
> *their needs, that it may benefit those who listen.*
>
> (Ephesians 4:29)

DEAR JESUS, it is my heart's desire that Your words will breathe life into myself and others. I pray that I would think before I speak and that I would fill my mind with the truth of Your Word. It's my heart's desire that the words of my mouth and the meditation of my heart will be pleasing to You. Thank You that through the Holy Spirit, I can be a person of life-giving words.

"Each person creates the life they live by choosing the words they speak."

— Thomas J. Powell

Day 7 is lovingly contributed by Ginger, whose life forever changed over a cup of coffee with Steve, the man of her dreams. When they met, Steve was a pastor, widower, and single dad to his young son, Isaiah (who had a diagnosis of autism). When the time came, Ginger joyfully said good-bye to her singleness and yes to marriage, full-time ministry, and motherhood. Ginger considers it her greatest honor to be called Mommy. The Ekholms currently live in Central Minnesota, where Steve pastors a growing church. You can follow the Ekholms' journey and find more of Ginger's writings on her blog, Unpacked Heart (www. unpackedheart.wordpress.com).

Day 7
STAY FOCUSED

We must focus on Jesus, the source and goal of our faith.
— Hebrews 12:2 (GW)

> ## Life Lesson: Keep Your Eyes on Jesus

The messages the world sends never seem to stop. "You're not enough!" "Do what feels good!" "Truth is relative." If we don't have our focus on God, it is very easy to get wrapped up in the wrong message. There was a time I was in a very crowded, noisy restaurant with a dear friend. It had been a while since we had seen each other, and she had a story to tell that I couldn't wait to hear! As I listened intently for the details of the story, I found myself hanging on her every word! It didn't seem to matter that the room was as noisy as it was because my focus was on my friend! Eventually, my attention began to drift from my friend to a conversation at a nearby table. I tried to refocus but sadly found myself interested in chatter that meant nothing to me. My friend was gracious when she realized I was distracted, but it was a powerful lesson for me to stay focused when listening.

In the same way, when we focus our eyes and our attention on Jesus, we posture our hearts to receive what He wants to say. Listen for His voice in your everyday life. Tune your heart to His Word so that you can always hear what He has to say to you. Spend time with Him as you would your best friend. Hold his promises deep in your heart. Let His every word be your deepest treasure.

May we always keep our eyes on Jesus, our hearts open to His Word and ready to listen and obey all He asks of us. In return, we will engage in the sweetest ongoing conversation this world has to offer. The best relationship you can ever have is with your Savior.

My sheep listen to my voice; I know them and they follow me.
(John 10:27, NLT)

HEAVENLY FATHER, Your voice is so sweet. Your heart for me is full of love. You have my best interest in mind, and Your Word is always true. Please help me to tune out all other voices and focus in on You. Open my eyes to see You and open my heart to hear You and listen to You. I fix my eyes on Jesus once again so that I can be ready to listen intently to Your every word and follow Your lead all of my days.

"Turn your eyes upon Jesus
Look full in His wonderful face.
And the things of earth will grow strangely dim,
in the light of His glory and grace."

— Helen H. Lemmel

BE JOYFUL IN HOPE
patience IN *affliction faithful* IN PRAYER

-Romans 12:12-

Day 8 is lovingly contributed by Dr. Wanda Walborn, who is currently in her thirteenth year as the director of spiritual formation at the Rockland County campus of Nyack College. Ron and Wanda are the parents of four children: Kelly (twenty-seven), Brice (25), Karis (24), and Karly (22). In her "free" time, she enjoys sports, reading, the outdoors, and-above all, spending time with her granddaughter, Bella (18 months), and grandson Ashton!

Day 8

CULTIVATE A LISTENING EAR

The shepherd walks right up to the gate. The gatekeeper opens the gate to him and the sheep recognize his voice. He calls his own sheep by name and leads them out. When he gets them all out, he leads them and they follow because they are familiar with his voice. They won't follow a stranger's voice but will scatter because they aren't used to the sound of it.

— Hebrews 12:2 (GW)

> ## Life Lesson: Hearing God's Voice

*A*s busy and as loud as our society is today, it is critical that you learn to be good listeners to the Lord. People will always try to talk you into things that don't seem right to you, and the pressure to join in will be very great. As long as you know the voice of God and choose to obey Him, you will be just fine.

The Sovereign Lord has given me a well-instructed tongue, to know the word that sustains the weary. He wakens me morning by morning, wakens my ear to listen like one being instructed. The Sovereign Lord has opened my ears; I have not been rebellious, I have not turned away.

(Isaiah 50:4–5)

When the Lord is waking you each morning to listen like a student, he has a very specific directive that He wants you to learn. You will need special focus and attentiveness to ensure that you receive what He is imparting. It is critical that you do not have selective hearing and only choose to listen to the parts you like. Isaiah 53:6 reads, "We all, like sheep, have gone astray, each of us has turned to his own way." All of us want to do our own thing and be independent, which is a part of growing and maturing; however, to turn away from God in rebellion will only lead to heartache and pain. He will let you go, but His desire is for you to trust His ways and believe what He tells you.

In John 10, Jesus tells a story of a good shepherd who opens the gate for his sheep, and they listen to him and follow him. They will never follow a stranger; in fact, they will run away from him because they don't recognize the stranger's voice. Stay close to Jesus so you can hear His voice no matter how softly He may speak.

FATHER, there are times when I don't listen to You because I want to do my own thing. I'm sorry for this attitude and ask that You help me want to listen to Your voice. I want to trust You and believe what You tell me.

"Many of us are choosing to live lives that do not set us up to pay attention, to notice those places where God is at work and to ask ourselves what these things mean. We long for a word from the Lord, but somehow we have been suckered into believing that the pace we keep is what leadership requires. We slide inexorably into a way of life that offers little or no opportunity for paying attention and then wonder why we are not hearing from God when we need God most."

— Ruth Haley Barton

I WILL WALK BY

faith

EVEN

WHEN I CAN'T

See

2 CORINTHIANS 5:1

Day 9 is lovingly contributed by Jessie Brookhart-Knost, who is a homeschooling mother of two children: her son, Grant (6), and daughter, Lexi (2). It is her supreme joy and blessing to be a mother, and she hopes to impart love and worship for the Lord in every aspect of life and in any circumstance.

Day 9
EXPECT TROUBLES

The crucible is for silver, and the furnace is for gold, and a man is tested by his praise.

— Proverbs 27:21 (ESV)

> **Life Lesson: Commit Your Heart to Praise God in Suffering**

My loves, my children, keep this truth close to your heart. This life will not be easy. You will be faced with troubles in this life. These trials might anger you, frustrate you, wear you out, depress you, discourage you, hurt you, grieve you, and even cost you your life. You may even be tempted to dangerously wonder how these things could happen if God truly loves you. But guard your hearts and minds from turning down this grievous road of thought! Such thinking is a product of the enemy. Instead, know that God only allows troubles because He loves you!

Troubles aren't pleasant. But our joy should never be derived from our circumstances. If we set our hearts on the mundane, the temporal, then we consign our hope to feeble circumstance. But if we instead set our hearts on the eternal, which is God's reward through Christ, then our hope rests on the very power of God, and we will always have joy with praise on our lips, notwithstanding any trial.

Earlier in my life, I faced trials that were on the verge of overcoming me. I was completely unprepared and spiritually immature, with no ability to fend off this spiritual onslaught. But I clung to the truth of my salvation through Jesus, which caused me to quickly realize that I was no longer content being ignorant of God's Word and spiritually immature. And so it was through the horrible suffering—which God, in His providence, allowed me to experience—that God gave me the sweet and great blessing of drawing me near to Him and assuring me that my faith was genuine. My deepest spiritual growth was forged through the painful trials that God allowed me to suffer.

> *[In your salvation and inheritance through Christ] you rejoice, though now for a little while, if necessary, you have been grieved by various trials, so that the tested genuineness of your faith— more precious than gold that perishes though it is tested by fire—may be found to result in the praise and glory and honor at the revelation of Jesus Christ.* (1 Peter 1:6–8, ESV)

DEAR FATHER IN HEAVEN, please let me understand that this life will have troubles. But please also grant me peace and wisdom to know that You work all things for the good of those who love You. Please root my heart in a deep love for You and Your Word. Use me as an instrument to instill praise of Your glorious character and name, no matter the circumstance. Please help me to love You in truth so that when others see me, it is not me they really see but You instead. Amen.

"When George Peabody was staying at Sir Charles Reed's house, he saw the youngest child bringing to his father a large Bible for family prayers. Mr. Peabody said, 'Ah! my boy, you carry the Bible now; but the time is coming when you will find that the Bible must carry you.'"

— Charles Haddon Spurgeon

not by my strength but his

- Zechariah 4:6 -

Day 10 is lovingly contributed by Michelle Post, who is an army wife and mother to seven children (both adopted and biological). As a wife and mother, she strives for a Micah 6:8 family—one that does justice, loves mercy, and walks humbly with God. She is also a Christian stylist and color consultant. She derives great joy from awakening women to their beautiful, flawless design. You can learn more about Michelle and her passion for revealing God's beauty at www.darlingbydesign.com.

Day 10
THE HERO'S SECRET

Consider it pure joy, my brothers and sisters, whenever you face trials of many kinds, because you know that the testing of your faith produces perseverance. Let perseverance finish its work so that you may be mature and complete, not lacking anything.

— James 1:2-4

> **Life Lesson: Persevere with Joy**

Think of your favorite childhood storybooks. What made them so captivating to you? Was it that Choco finally found his mama? Was it that the little red caboose was finally able to prove his worth and be recognized? Did you dream of being like David defeating the bully Goliath? Could you relate to Sister Bear learning how to work her troubles out with Lizzy Bruin? Maybe it was learning that Ferdinand the Bull was happy to be who he was created to be, even if it didn't seem normal to anyone else. Almost every good story sees the hero overcome someone or something that at first seemed impossible. Let me suggest you were drawn to those books because, in the end, those characters overcame their trials.

My darling children, you will face troubles, heartache, and be temped to quit, but don't give up. Your story isn't over yet. You've already begun experiencing tough times, and they will continue throughout your life.

But look at what you've already overcome—having block towers and sand castles stomped on by others, saying good-bye to best friends, moving a lot, the death of a beloved grandpa, responsibility to care for others who aren't like you, feeling lonely and at times rejected, feeling misunderstood by everyone around you, etc. I want to challenge you to keep trying with a joyful heart in those hard times because your story isn't over yet. Every hero faces great challenges and trials, but the Bible makes it clear that troubles can be good for us! Through faith, persevering in trials makes you complete in Christ.

When you face challenges, you are given the opportunity to overcome! You have the chance to persevere and see how God can be your strength. If you don't accept the challenge to persevere, you will shrink back and wither up. If you muster up the courage to keep going, God will make your heart strong and complete, having all you need! In our home, we always talk about (1) walking with God, (2) being kind, and (3) doing the right thing. When you persevere in your walk with God, you cannot help but be kind and do the right thing. And never forget:

I can do everything through Him who gives me strength.
(Philippians 4:13)

DEAR GOD, thank You for allowing me to experience trials so I can grow stronger, increase my faith, and become complete. Help me when I want to quit. Remind me to be joyful when I want to scream and cry. You are my good and faithful God, and I trust what the Bible says that if I want to be strong, I have to keep persevering.

"Our greatest weakness lies in giving up. The most certain way to succeed is always to try just one more time."
— Thomas A. Edison

Day 11 is lovingly contributed by Jessica Serrano, who currently resides in sunny Palm Harbor, Florida. She has the privilege of doing laundry for five, including her 4-year-old princess, 2-year-old perpetually dirty son, and their newest addition, a beautiful eight-year-old girl. During nap times, she enjoys creating for Ink and Light Lettering, speaking to groups in the community, perfecting the art of cooking with almond flour, helping her husband run their Maximized Health Clinic, Ignite Chiropractic and Wellness, and listening to educational TED Talks in preparation for the charter school she is opening in 2018. You can find Jessica on Facebook at Ink and Light Lettering or on Instagram at JessSerrano.

Day 11

BY FAITH (INSERT YOUR NAME HERE)

*These were all commended for their faith, yet none of them received what had been promised, since God had planned something better for us so that [**only together with us**] would they be made perfect.*

— Hebrews 11:39–40

> ## Life Lesson: Live Out Your Faith

*I*f there was ever a chapter in the Bible that is literally bursting at the seams, it's Hebrews 11 (go ahead, put down this book, open your Bible, and soak that chapter in for a minute). God packed so much in there you feel about ten pounds heavier after digesting all the power and goodness expressed in those lines. From Abel to Rahab, the author highlights so many key players he doesn't even "have time" to talk about people like Gideon and David! Imagine that. Then, of course, there is the mention of creation, the parting of the Red Sea, and the fall of Jericho, just to name a few. And why are all these powerhouse leaders and world-changing events squeezed into forty verses? God says it in two words: **by faith**.

The words **by faith** appear over twenty times in this chapter alone. The author's emphasis is not on belief but rather on **behavior**. These stories are about how faith was **lived** out. As I took a closer look at the "heroes of the faith" mentioned in the chapter and their stories of faith, what I found made me step back for a minute. None of them were commended for the sort of things I so desperately seek recognition for. It wasn't about their law-keeping abilities and how well they obeyed. It wasn't about their earthly popularity and being well-liked. It wasn't about their success as they climbed up the achievement ladder. It had everything to do with **surrender** and **trust**. Their faith walk was raw and radical and eerily similar to the life of that baby born in a manger.

So here is where you and I come in. I think there is a missing verse. Let's call it Hebrews 11:38 ½, and it's where your story fits in. Just like Noah and Abraham, you have a specific calling. At some point, you will be presented with an opportunity to step out of a boat in a raging storm. From my own experience and from reading the stories of those who came before me, I have come to the conclusion that these acts of surrender and trust are never easy or comfortable. Thank goodness it has never been about me and my sufficiency, and your faith verse won't be about you either. Sing the song of **God's faithfulness**. Insert your name after verse 38 and see where God is leading you today.

> *Remember your leaders, who spoke the word of God to you. Consider the outcome of their way of life and imitate their faith. Jesus Christ is the same yesterday and today and forever.* (Hebrews 13:7–8)

DEAR JESUS, the Perfecter of our faith, there has never been, and will never be, a more beautiful story than the one You are writing. I know it is not about my efforts today but about what You've already done. Jehovah God, please lead me in today's faith walk.

"Take the first step in faith. You don't have to see the whole staircase, just take the first step."

— Martin Luther King Jr.

Give thanks TO THE Lord FOR HE IS GOOD HIS love ENDURES forever

— Psalm 107:1 —

Day 12 is lovingly contributed by Maria Shepherd, who is married to Pastor Greg Shepherd, and they have a twelve-year-old son, Caleb. As a family, they are missionaries living and serving in Haiti. Their main focus is to reach the children of Haiti for Christ, educate them, and give them the faith, hope, and confidence they need to create sustainable change in their country. If you are interested in contributing to their ministry or doing a missions trip to Haiti, you can learn more at http://www.rtsmissions.com.

Day 12
STANDING FIRM

Be watchful, stand firm in the faith, be courageous, be strong.

— 1 Corinthians 16:13 (RSV)

⟩ Life Lesson: Be Bold and Courageous in Your Faith ⟨

My child, as you continue to grow and learn about life, I want you to remember to be bold and courageous, standing firm in your faith. Many things are going to come your way and try to break your boldness. They will make you question your courage. People may knock you down with their words or actions. Trials will come and may make you think you can't handle any more. You must stand strong, be bold and courageous through it all, knowing that, with Christ, you will endure.

I have faced many trials in my life, some before I knew Christ and some since making Him Lord of my life. I can tell you that it is much easier to face those trials with Christ. When we are bold and courageous in our faith, we are able to accomplish so much more for His glory. It doesn't mean that following Christ will make our life a piece of cake and we won't endure trials. However, it does mean that we will be able to call on Him to give us the courage and boldness we need.

No matter the size or strength of the trials I have faced, God has never let me down. He has been there to encourage me and give me the strength and boldness I needed to endure. I pray that you too will find this same comfort in knowing that He will provide your strength and boldness. You need only ask and seek guidance from His Word.

> *This book of the law shall not depart out of your mouth, but you shall meditate on it day and night, that you may be careful to do according to all that is written in it; for then you shall make your way prosperous, and then you shall have good success. Have I not commanded you? Be strong and of good courage; be not frightened, neither be dismayed; for the LORD your God is with you wherever you go.*

(Joshua 1:8–9, RSV)

HEAVENLY FATHER, please help me to always keep Your Word in my heart and mind that it will be the source of my strength and boldness. May I always look to You to find my help. You alone are my strength and my shield. Help me to live boldly and courageously that I might be a light for Your kingdom.

"The remedy for discouragement is the Word of God. When you feed your heart and mind with its truth, you regain your perspective and find renewed strength."

— Warren Wiersbe

WITH God,
all things are
possible
-math 19:26-

Day 13 is lovingly contributed by Melati Minter, who was born in Indiana but has lived most of her life in Florida. She surrendered her life to Jesus Christ in 1999, right after graduating from the University of Florida. It was at the University of Florida where she met her husband, Michael. They've been married for fourteen years and are blessed with three children: Claire (twelve), Joel (ten), and Grace (two). Through a women's Bible study and training ministry called The Well, Melati discovered and has developed her spiritual gifts, as well as come to understand how to carry out the Great Commission mandate to disciple others. Melati is a freelance graphic designer and a homeschool mom. She loves crafting, reading, learning new recipes, and traveling with her family.

Day 13

REJOICE IN THE LORD ALWAYS

Blessed be the Lord, who daily loads us with benefits, the God of our salvation! Selah.

— Psalm 68:19 (NKJV)

> ### Life Lesson: Live a Life of Thanksgiving

The greatest lesson I can give you is to remember to live a life of thanksgiving. It is easy to come up with a short list of reasons to be thankful, but taking time to reflect on the multitude of things the Lord has given you and expressing gratitude to Him will require discipline.

Each day is a gift meant to be enjoyed and celebrated with a joyful heart. Every day is loaded with treasures from our Lord's loving hands— from simple joys such as food that fills your belly, a welcoming hug, an encouraging word from another, to the delight in hearing children's laughter, the sweet smell of flowers, witnessing a perfectly painted pastel sky, and everything in between! The list is absolutely endless.

And not only does the Lord graciously give you these daily benefits, most importantly, He offers you a relationship with Himself. This relationship He offers trumps all of our Lord's gifts. Beginning here on this earth and continuing through eternity, this relationship is the ultimate gift. It is to be remembered and offered up in praise.

Because there will be days when you're walking through trials, it will be hard to be thankful consistently. But remember that He is worthy of your praise. He's good, His plan is perfect, and He promises you His presence through every challenging season.

Having a thankful heart will remind you of God's goodness, His undeniable care for each area of your life, and the increasing desire He has for you to know Him and trust Him with everything. I have learned that no time is ever wasted spent in prayer thanking God. Rather, that time has been invaluable for shaping my character, giving me a proper perspective on circumstances and building my trust.

So my desire is for you to take the time and thank the Lord for everything—often and continuously and in all circumstances. Live a life of thanksgiving. May you have a heart of thanksgiving that overflows into your conversations and into how you treat others. May it be a powerful display of your overwhelming gratitude to God.

> *So then, just as you received Christ Jesus as Lord, continue to live your lives in him, rooted and built up in him, strengthened in the faith as you were taught, and overflowing with thankfulness.* (Colossians 2:6–7)

DEAR HEAVENLY FATHER, thank You so much for everything You have lovingly given me. Thank You for filling every single day with blessings beyond measure for me to enjoy. Above all, thank You for giving me an everlasting relationship with You. Please help me to remember to express gratitude for all things and in all situations. May I live a life of thanksgiving so others will be drawn to You.

"The mature Christian offers not just polite thanks but heartfelt thanks that springs from a far deeper source than his own pleasure. Thanksgiving is a spiritual exercise, necessary to the building of a healthy soul. It takes us out of the stuffiness of ourselves into the fresh breeze and sunlight of the will of God. The simple act of thanking Him is for most of us an abrupt change of activity, a break from work and worry, a move toward re-creation."

— Elisabeth Elliot

Day 14 is lovingly contributed by Heather Gilstrap, who is a blessed woman and is married to Griffin, who is the youth pastor at Harborside Church. And she is the mama to three sweet little girls, Harper Grace, Paisley Joy, and Skyler Faith! She loves soccer, chocolate, and worship. Her desire is to make art and inspire others to live a life that is lovely and free. You can find more about her on her website, http://www.lovelyandfree.net/.

Day 14

BE YOU

I praise you because I am fearfully and wonderfully made;
your works are wonderful, I know that full well.

— Psalm 139:14

Life Lesson: Have Confidence

*I*f I could teach you just one thing, it would be confidence. Be brave and fearless in who you are! Because who you are is designed by the Designer, created by the Creator, and perfectly hand-made by the Maker.

Don't you see? You could try to be other people, imitations, copies of— but what God has given you, no one can take, so don't hide it, don't mask it. Embrace who you are, every detail on the inside and the outside. Embrace your personality, the way you feel, your determination, your fight, your peaceful heart, your abilities, and your creativity.

And the way you embrace all of who you are is through seeking Him. The more you seek Jesus, the more you find yourself. The more you study His Word, spend time with Him, and worship Him, the more He shows you who you are and who you were created to be. You stop seeing yourself through the eyes of others, and He starts revealing your true identity to you. This is an identity that has been bought with a price, a heart that is being sought after, and a soul that has been destined to be in a relationship with our Savior.

This world will tell you to fit into a mold of beauty or a standard of success. But you…you have something in you that is irreplaceable and that is undeniable. It's striking. And how do we respond? With thanks, with a grateful heart. You are loved by a perfect God who made you piece by piece. So with the breath in your lungs that He gave you, praise Him and be confident in our Heavenly Father and in how He made you and in the calling He has on your life.

This life is hard. And there will be many rough moments and amazing days, but always remember who you are in Christ. Walk in this confidence, walk in this truth. You are a child of God. When He is by your side and if you keep your eyes on Him, He will keep His hand upon you.

> *For we are God's handiwork, created in Christ Jesus to do*
> *good works, which God prepared in advance for us to do.*
> (Ephesians 2:10)

FATHER, Your ways are perfect. Your love is flawless. Thank You for how You love me, delight in me, and how You have created me. Who am I to judge what is good, to judge the works of Your hands? Lord, teach me to look at myself and see what You see. I know You have created me for a purpose and that You have a calling on my life. I desire for my confidence to be found in You that I am not shaken by the ways of this world and how I am seen, but that I know who I am and I find all of myself in You. May praise and thankfulness be on my lips. Lord, I choose today to be confident and walk in Your Truth.

"Be who you are, not who the world wants you to be."
— Anonymous

Day 15 is lovingly contributed by Cheryl Moore, who is passionate about Christ's love for her and is crazy about her husband and their seven children ranging from three to sixteen years of age. Homeschooling, organic gardening, cooking, reading, photography, and the fine arts keep each day overflowing. While striving to be a faithful steward, she is learning to embrace the adventure the Lord has planned for her and loves encouraging others along the way.

Day 15

YOUR GENERATION

Now when David had served God's purpose in his own generation, he fell asleep.

— Acts 13:36

> ### Life Lesson: Allow God to Use Your Passion for His Purpose

This is a fascinating verse about one of the most passionate characters in the Bible. God used David's personality, skills, and gifts for His glory; and in spite of this man's many shortcomings, God declared that he was a man after His own heart. What set David apart? Perhaps it was his integrity. Or maybe it correlated with how quickly he repented from sin. But his passionate pursuit of God and willingness to do whatever He wanted definitely had something to do with it.

You have been given specific characteristics and gifts that are a reflection of God. He was intentional in your design. You were also created with a specific mission to fulfill. Your generation needs the Gospel now, and God has chosen you to be His hands and feet. The passionate pursuit of God is where you will discover your fulfillment. There is no time to indulge in sinful desires or play games with the world. Ephesians 5:15–16 urgently pleads for you to be very "careful how you live making the most of every opportunity, for the days are evil."

Do whatever it takes to remain passionate in your pursuit of Him. Set aside every distraction and hindrance, just like the writer admonished in

83

Hebrews 12:1, so that you will be able to run the race with perseverance. The obstacles on the path you will journey are guaranteed to be difficult, perhaps humanly impossible. But as long as you keep your eyes laser-focused on the Author and Perfector of your faith, the Lover of your soul, your passion will remain. And the fire that stirs in your heart will motivate your actions, even when it feels most challenging!

Can you imagine what David must have felt like when he heard the words, "Well done, good and faithful servant" (Matthew 25:21)? Honor your Heavenly Father with your talents and skills. Use them for His glory. Ecclesiastes 9:10 instructs, "Whatever your hands find to do, do it with all your might." And "seek first His kingdom" (Matthew 6:33). He will take care of everything else. Keep that fire burning brightly so that you, like David, will be used for His purpose in the generation that is watching you and seeking the true light. You have a destiny to fulfill!

Never be lacking in zeal, but keep your spiritual fervor, serving the Lord. (Romans 12:11)

DEAR FATHER GOD, please grow my passion for You. Let it pour out into my choices and actions so that I will honor You. May the fire that burns brightly in me spread to my generation so that Your Word will be proclaimed and Your name glorified. Fulfill your purpose for my life as I learn to passionately pursue You.

"God's purpose for my life was that I have a passion for God's glory and that I have a passion for my joy in that glory, and that these two are one passion."

— Jonathan Edwards

I CAN DO ALL Things THROUGH Christ WHO strengthens ME

- philippians 4:13 -

Day 16 is lovingly contributed by Jenna, who is a homeschool mama of four (with two in heaven) residing in Alaska with her husband Michael, and two dogs. She is passionate about health, wellness, a good cup of coffee, and encouraging others to use the gifts God has given them.

Day 16
GRACE

But he said to me, "My grace is sufficient for you, for my power is made perfect in weakness." Therefore I will boast all the more gladly about my weaknesses, so that Christ's power may rest on me.

— 2 Corinthians 12:9

> ## Life Lesson: Remember, Grace

I remember moments in my young married life when I could not understand why, when I had done everything "right," God would possibly allow me to go through more hard times. I had endured quite a few and thought it might be my time for reprieve, but life does not work that way. For years, I truly felt God had abandoned me, but I knew deep down inside it was not true. I wondered if I had done something that made Him withhold His grace and love. There were days I looked up at the stars longingly. The love and deep relationship I once had seemed like it was missing, and I could not figure out why.

He is Jehovah Shammah (the Lord is there). God did not abandon Israel, and He would not abandon me. He was there with me. **Grace**.

In these trying years, you all were born, and there were days I felt like I had nothing to give you. When I listened, He would whisper, "My grace is sufficient for you." There were times I struggled with why God would even bless me with you when I felt so unworthy and ill-equipped, struggling to be a good mom and feeling like I had failed. And He would gently speak, "My power is made perfect in weakness."

In my darkest years, God taught me a lot through you. He taught me of His extravagant love. It is one thing to know God, but without the tests and the trials, you never truly have to live your faith. "Now Faith is the substance of things hoped for, the evidence of things not seen" (Hebrews 11:1, NKJV).

The days I was most fragile, I would look into your eyes and see that, like you, I was still growing. Just as you were growing and I was gracious with you, He was, in the same way, gracious with me. He did not have to give me grace. He did not need to reach down and open my eyes. He loves me in spite of myself. And therein lies the joy! **Grace**.

As I look at the world we live in, I see that there is no shelter that exists to keep you from hardships. You will endure them, and if there is anything I long for you to know, it is that He is there for you. He never said He would take away our pain in this life; He endured pain. He never said He would protect us from hardships; He walks with us through them. He tells us in His Word that "in this world, we will have troubles, but to take heart; He has overcome the world" (paraphrased from John 16:33).

When troubles come, I want you to remember to "consider it pure joy whenever you face trials of many kinds because the testing of your faith produces perseverance. Perseverance must finish its work so you may be mature, complete, and not lacking anything (James 1:2–4 paraphrased)." Trials are what grow us! You will face them. You will be tested. You have the opportunity to grow. **Grace**.

When you struggle to know what to do, seek His face. When I struggled, my mom would say , "Pray for wisdom. God promises He will give it." El

HaNe'eman—the faithful God—will be faithful to you. He is not looking in our times of trials to point out what we have done wrong. He gives us wisdom freely out of His love. **Grace.**

If any of you lacks wisdom, you should ask God, who gives generously to all without finding fault, and it will be given to you. (James 1:5)

DEAR FATHER, when I am struggling in life, help me to seek You for wisdom. Show me Your goodness and faithfulness in the midst of and in spite of my circumstances. Help me to know Your grace in my life that I will not be swayed but rooted firmly in You. Establish my steps, and as I seek Your wisdom, thank You for giving it freely. In Jesus' name, amen.

"If God is able to make everything that happens to us work together for our good, then ultimately everything that happens to us is good. We must be careful to use the word ultimately. On the earthly plane things that happen to us may indeed be evil… Yet God in His goodness transcends all these things and works them out to our good. For the Christian, ultimately, there are no tragedies."

— R.C. Sproul

Day 17 is lovingly contributed by Paige Eavenson, who is a wife, a homeschooling mompreneur, and lover of all things chocolate. She does like to work off the calories by exercising daily and encouraging others to do the same. Paige, her husband Clay, and four children—Cade, Claire, Caris, and Corrie—are currently on an adventure in South Carolina. Her youngest daughter, Corrie, is a survivor of the rare liver disease biliary atresia through the gift of a liver transplant. Paige is passionate about encouraging other families in the liver disease world and speaking on the importance of organ donation.

Follow her adventures and get to know her better on Facebook, Instagram, or at www.paigeeavenson.com.

Day 17

THE BEST IS YET TO COME

*No eye has seen, no ear has heard, and no mind has
imagined what God has prepared for those who love Him.*
— 1 Corinthians 2:9 (NLT)

> ## Life Lesson: Have Faith for the Days Ahead

One of the greatest gifts I want to leave you with is the gift of faith. When going through this life, you are going to have good days and bad days. In the good days, it is easy to be hopeful and expectant of great things to come. However, some days you are going to get news that will disappoint you, frustrate you, and make you want to throw in the towel on this thing called life.

That's where faith comes in. Just like the seasons change during the year, so will your circumstances change if you only have a little faith and believe the best is yet to come. In the winter months, it tends to get darker out earlier, it's colder, and the trees look dead and lifeless. We all know that winter doesn't last forever, and pretty soon, spring is in the air. The trees start to blossom again, the sun shines a little longer each day, and new life seems to spring forth everywhere.

The same is true in your life. Some seasons will be dark, lonely, and cold. You will be tempted to isolate yourself and hibernate from your friends and family and community. It will be tough to see that anything good can come from such a frustrating time. However, if you will take that mustard seed of faith and plant it in your mind and thoughts, then water it with the Word of God on a daily basis, in time it will bring forth new life.

New dreams, visions, hopes, and goals are all birthed out of a seed of faith. When I was given the opportunity to start fresh in a new city with new friends, it was a little scary at first. The details of how it all would come to pass were daunting. I knew, however, God didn't give us a spirit of fear but a measure of faith. He went before us and prepared a way. He was just waiting for us to step out in faith and follow Him until we could see the blessings right in front of us. It didn't take long to start seeing God in every person we met and every circumstance He placed us in. Nothing happens by accident when God is your tour guide. He wants to show you places that will blow your mind and introduce you to people who will change your life forever. You only have to step out in faith and believe **the best is yet to come**.

> ***Now faith is confidence in what we hope for and assurance about what we do not see.*** (Hebrews 11:1)

DEAR HEAVENLY FATHER, please grow my faith and give me confidence to hope for what I cannot see. I pray I will not plant seeds of doubt and discouragement but rather seeds of faith, hope, and love. Lead me in the way You want me to go and show me whom I can bless along the journey. May You, Lord, always be my tour guide and help me to hear Your voice leading me down the path I need to take next. I trust, Father, that my steps are ordered by You. Help me to reach out to You when I am afraid. Bless the works of my hands, Lord, as I use them to serve You and bring glory to Your name.

"Never be afraid to trust an unknown future to a known God."

— Corrie ten Boom

Because Your STEADFAST ♥ LOVE is better than Life My lips will PRAISE you

Psalm 63:3

Day 18 is lovingly contributed by Carrie Ann Dressler, who—along with her husband, Scot—has been serving as an international worker with the Christian and Missionary Alliance in Palestine/Israel since 2004. She is the mother of five awesome third-culture kids: Thomas, Maggie, Scoty, Georgia Kate, and Charlotte. She is known for her boisterous, heartfelt laugh and welcoming smile. She loves scrapbooking, singing (especially Broadway show tunes—loudly), and engaging in relationship with those around her.

Day 18

HARD PRESSED ON EVERY SIDE

We are hard pressed on every side, but not crushed;
perplexed, but not in despair; persecuted, but not
abandoned; struck down, but not destroyed.
— 2 Corinthians 4:8–9

Life Lesson: Do Not Fear

*G*uns pointed at you. Angry crowds running toward you and away from soldiers shooting teargas and rubber slugs over you. A frustrated soldier threatening to shoot us. A furious crowd mobbing a parked car. "Get down on the floor and tuck your head under your arms!" I shouted in our car during our commute home from school. I am dismayed to acknowledge that these are our realities. How easy it would be for us to wallow in fear—to be controlled by a fear that threatens to grip our hearts and minds. Yet in the face of danger and the unknown, how I desire for you to cling to the promises of our strong and mighty God.

> **So do not fear, for I am with you; do not be dismayed, for I am your God. I will strengthen you and help you; I will uphold you with my righteous right hand.** (Isaiah 41:10)

This life has not been easy. We stand as cultural outsiders, as foreigners in a land that is not our own. We stand between two very distinct and often opposing cultures: Palestinian and Israeli. Some days, I have asked myself if the sacrifice has been too great, the toll on your hearts and lives too much. God patiently reminds me that when He called your father and me, He also called you our children. In the times of great fear and persecution, when a young friend (recently baptized) dies a violent death, when another friend is forced to leave his village under threat of his life, or in any of the aforementioned situations, God has been our rock and our salvation. "Truly my soul finds rest in God; my salvation comes from him. Truly he is my rock and my salvation; he is my fortress, I will never be shaken." (Psalm 62:1–2).

There is nothing that can separate you from the love of God that is in Christ Jesus. As you face the future, the unknown, walk in the assurance of God's constant presence with you. When challenges threaten to overwhelm you, remember that though you are hard-pressed on every side, you are not crushed. And when fear wraps its arms around you with a stranglehold that you feel powerless to fight, know that you are not abandoned to walk this life alone.

> *For I am convinced that neither death nor life, neither angels nor demons, neither the present nor the future, nor any powers, neither height nor depth, nor anything else in all creation, will be able to separate us from the love of God that is in Christ Jesus our Lord.* (Romans 8:38–39)

It is in His strength that we stand. It is in His strength that we conquer. It is in His strength that we reach a lost and dying world with the love and salvation of Jesus.

O GOD, our rock and our salvation, help us to face life in Your strength. Do not allow us to wallow in our worries and fears. Call us out of the mud and mire of our own anxiety and set our feet on Your rock! Help us to walk in the victory of Your salvation. Use us, even in our weaknesses, to reach the lost with the compassion, love, and mercy of Your Son. Put within us a desire to know You more deeply, intimately acquainting ourselves with Your presence and sufferings, even in the most fearful of circumstances. O God, be our strength and shield. Raise up in our children men and women of faith who stand on Your promises for the sake of the world and Your gospel.

"If the Lord be with us, we have no cause of fear. His eye is upon us, His arm over us, His ear open to our prayer—His grace sufficient, His promise unchangeable."

— John Newton

Day 19 is lovingly contributed by Susan Brennan, who is a marriage and family therapist and lives with her husband, a semi-retired carpenter in Northern Minnesota. Together, and with God's instruction, they raised three sons. All came to a saving knowledge of the Lord Jesus and are now married and raising sons and daughters of their own.

Day 19

BRAVE CHILDREN HOLD GOD'S HAND

Fear not, for I am with you; be not dismayed, for I am your God; I will strengthen you, I will help you, I will uphold you with my righteous right hand.

— Isaiah 41:10 (ESV)

Life Lesson: Take Courage

My greatest mission, as your mother, was to impart living faith in Jesus Christ to your young spirits and to demonstrate His desire to have a close personal relationship with you. His desire is to give you confidence and peace, even in the midst of uncertainty. He does not push His children into life's arena. He holds your hand. His gentleness will be your strength always. He is moved at the sound of your voice, and He will never leave you.

Like most mothers, I wanted to convey unconditional love and self-sacrifice to beautify the path of God for my children. Reality entered the first time I stayed up most of the night walking a colicky baby. A friend and seasoned mother of seven children offered wise advice and helped me reposition my role in this great task. She said what a child most needs in a mother is a mother who needs Jesus. Now that I knew I could model!

Children come into this world looking for someone who is looking for them and soon come to recognize their mother's face. Hers is the face that will not go away. Mothers are that first mirror in which children see their own reflection. Nighttime cries are sometimes a longing, not for food but for assurance that darkness cannot erase that face of love. My failures will never obscure His light, for His strength is made perfect in our weakness. His light never dims. He never grows weary and never falls asleep. He is God of the day and God of the night.

> *For I, the LORD your God, hold your right hand; it is I who say to you, "Fear not, I am the one who helps you."*

(Isaiah 41:13, ESV)

O LORD, open the understanding of these precious children's hearts! Cause them to know You, to see Your love in my eyes, to see Your comfort through my touch, and to trust in Your Son, Jesus Christ, for the forgiveness of sin and promise of eternal life. And for those many occasions when I am weary and fall short of the mark, give them faith to believe in Your unfailing love. You alone can save! Shine, Jesus, shine, and bring my children into Your kingdom!

"Are you there too, Sir?" said Edmund. "I am," said Aslan. "But there I have another name. You must learn to know me by that name. This was the very reason why you were brought to Narnia, that by knowing me here for a little, you may know me better there."

— C. S. Lewis

Seek first the kingdom of God

MATTHEW 6:33

Day 20 is lovingly contributed by KC Newbill, who grew up in Nashville, Tennessee, and married her high school sweetheart. She has been married for almost twenty-four years. She has two great college-aged kids. They all live in Tampa, Florida, where her husband is a children's pastor. God has taught her many lessons about Himself through their animals. They have two horses, two dogs, one cat, two parakeets, and eight chickens. One day, she hopes to live on a farm and add many more animals to their family so that God can continue to reveal Himself to her through them!

Day 20

HIDE AND SEEK

You will seek me and find me, when you seek me with all your heart.

— Jeremiah 29:13 (ESV)

> **Life Lesson: Seek Him While He May Be Found**

*E*verybody loves a good game of hide-and-seek. My children are in college now. They are twenty-one and twenty. We started playing hide-and-seek when they were preschoolers, and they still love to play. Just a few months ago, my son came home late one night with a few of his friends and told me and my husband that they wanted us to play a game of hide-and-seek with them. We looked at each other and laughed—and then we played. It was so much fun! We turned off all the lights and played in the dark. It is quite a thrill to be the seeker. You know the others are hiding, but finding them can often be a challenge!

We have a Creator who knows His creation! He created us in our mother's wombs (read Psalm 139). He knows that we like to play. He has asked us to play the greatest game of "hide-and-seek" ever. You might be asking, what is she talking about? Well, look at this verse. In Jeremiah 29:13, God says, "You will seek me and find me, when you seek me with all your heart" (ESV).

God has promised us that if we seek Him with our whole heart, we will find Him! That is the best thing we could choose to do with our time. I can't think of a better thing to devote my whole heart to than seeking Him. As a mom, there is nothing I love more from my kids than to see them seeking God with their whole hearts. There are so many things in this world that want to take our attention. Seeking Him is a game that we should definitely be playing! He's not really hiding—He is everywhere. He is hiding in plain sight and wants to be found, but we are easily distracted.

When we play at our house, we turn off all the lights, and the seeker has a flashlight. This makes it very easy to stay focused on the game. We need to turn off the lights to the distractions in our lives that keep us from seeking God with our whole heart.

Your next question may be, How do I seek God? First, start by asking Him to seek and search you. He already knows where you are—there is nowhere you can go to hide from Him! I encourage you to ask God to search your heart just like David did in Psalm 139:23–24: "Search me, O God, and know my heart; test my thoughts. Point out anything you find in me that makes you sad, and lead me along the path of everlasting life" (TLB).

Then, after you know your heart is fully focused on Him, ask Him to show Himself to you and start looking for Him everywhere. If you seek Him with your whole heart, you will find Him. What are you waiting for? Start searching!

DEAR LORD GOD, thank You for creating me in my mother's womb. Thank You for making me perfect—just the way You wanted. Please search my heart and test my thoughts. Please remove anything that is not fully focused on You. Please help me to find You. Help me to stay focused on seeking You. I look forward to finding You today! Thank You for promising to be found! In Jesus' name, amen.

"You will learn much about God, His Word, His purposes, and His ways as you spend time with Him. You will come to know Him during the day as you experience Him working in and through your life. Learning about Him is not, however, why you should want to have a quiet time with Him. The more you know Him and experience His love, the more you will love Him. Then you will want that time alone with Him because you do love Him and enjoy His fellowship."

— Henry T. Blackaby, Claude V. King, and Richard Blackaby

A NOTE FROM SARAH

The next ten devotionals are written by myself (Sarah Malanowski), author of the **Victorious Living Collection**. They come from the ten family mottos we have in our home. Please feel free to go to my resource page at Godisalwaysfaithful.com/resources/ to download your copy of these mottos to use in your home. Our children will be better stewards of God's Word and the gifts they have been given if we teach them how to follow the Lord's heart. That was the desire of my husband and me as we sat down to create the top ten things we want our sons to learn before they leave our home. I pray these devotionals will bless and encourage you. May they equip your family to live out their God-given potential!

Day 21

MAKE THE MOST OF EVERY OPPORTUNITY

Be very careful, then, how you live—not as unwise but as wise, making the most of every opportunity, because the days are evil.

— Ephesians 5:15–16

> ### Life Lesson: Maximize Your Moments

*E*very moment we receive in life can be enjoyed to the fullest, or it can be squandered. We squander our moments by being distracted and not focused on what God has given us. My children, I pray that you will embrace every moment that God gives you. I pray that you will find joy in the midst of the storms as you focus on who God is and not what your circumstances say to you. I pray that you will embrace the sweet moments that God gives to you.

Please don't waste your time wishing for someone else's moment. God is giving you the moments He wants you to cherish and celebrate. Every moment you have is a gift from Him, a gift that you can unwrap and cherish for the rest of your life. You are faced with a choice every day to embrace the moments that you are given or live your life wishing for the next moment.

I promise you that nothing bad lasts forever. Even your most difficult moments will pass. So while you are in them, find a way to embrace what God wants to teach you through them. Our lives are made up of moments, too many moments to count. I pray that you will embrace the sweet moments, allowing them to make you more like Christ and increase in you an ability to be a sweet aroma to those around you. I pray that you will treasure the difficult moments as in those moments, your spiritual muscles are being stretched and developed so you can be all that God has called you to be.

> *Consider it nothing but joy, my brothers and sisters, whenever you fall into various trials. Be assured that the testing of your faith [through experience] produces endurance [leading to spiritual maturity, and inner peace]. And let endurance have its perfect result and do a thorough work, so that you may be perfect and completely developed [in your faith], lacking in nothing.* (James 1:2–4, AMP)

DEAR FATHER GOD, please give me the strength to embrace every moment that You give me. May I never take a single moment for granted but may I cherish it for all that it is. Lord, You are the Author of my moments. May I honor You in how I spend them, and may I never wish for the moments that aren't mine to have. I pray that I will maximize every moment that You give me and find greater joy in You than anything else.

"I wish it need not have happened in my time," said Frodo. "So do I," said Gandalf, "and so do all who live to see such times. But that is not for them to decide. All we have to decide is what to do with the time that is given us."

— J. R. R. Tolkien, The Fellowship of the Ring

Day 22

BECOME A GRACE DISPENSER

*Make every effort to live in peace with all men and to be
holy; without holiness no one will see the Lord.*

— Hebrews 12:14

Life Lesson: Always Show Grace

We live in a world that is ready to judge you at any minute and any turn of life. God wants us to be dispensers of grace in a world gone crazy. Please don't wait for your friends to show you grace before you start showing it. I want you to be the trendsetter when it comes to grace. You are so beautiful, my child, and have so much to offer this world through the life that you live for God. That all starts with dispensing grace to those you come in contact with on a daily basis.

People are going to rub you the wrong way at times. You aren't going to get along with everyone a hundred percent of the time. But I ask you to show grace. When you are wronged or when someone hurts you, please give them the benefit of the doubt. Live a life of showing grace to everyone you come in contact with. As you set the pace and trend to be a grace dispenser, you will find that grace is poured out freely on you as well. That's the beauty of grace: you give grace to others, and it comes back to you in full measure.

We have experienced the unlimited beauty of God's grace on our lives. It's a privilege to show this grace to others. You are given the choice every day to dispense grace or judgment. I promise you that as you learn to dispense the grace that God has so lavishly poured out on your life, you will find yourself filled up. You will find that your days are full, your heart is joyful, and life has meaning. God, the Giver of grace, is giving you an opportunity every day to share in the wonder of dispensing grace to all those you come in contact with.

> *And God is able to make all grace [every favor and earthly blessing] come in abundance to you, so that you may always [under all circumstances, regardless of the need] have complete sufficiency in everything [being completely self-sufficient in Him], and have an abundance for every good work and act of charity.* (2 Corinthians 9:8, AMP)

DEAR FATHER GOD, please teach me what it means to be a dispenser of grace. May my first inclination in every situation I face be one of dispensing grace to others. May I never forget the grace that has so lavishly been poured out on my life, and may I freely pour this grace out to others I come in contact with.

"A man can no more take in a supply of grace for the future than he can eat enough today to last him for the next 6 months, nor can he inhale sufficient air into his lungs with one breath to sustain life for a week to come. We are permitted to draw upon God's store of grace from day to day as we need it."

— Dwight L. Moody

Day 23

THE ART OF LISTENING

*Understand this, my beloved brothers and sisters. Let every-
one be quick to hear [be a careful, thoughtful listener], slow
to speak [a speaker of carefully chosen words and], slow to
anger [patient, reflective, forgiving].*

— James 1:19 (AMP)

> ### Life Lesson: Listen Carefully

I cannot begin to tell you how many times I have missed something
important because I didn't slow down to listen. Yes, it would appear
that I was hearing what was said, but hearing and listening are two
different things. I can hear all sorts of things in a day, but until I stop
to listen with ears that are attentive and a heart that is ready to respond, it becomes just a passing statement.

My children, please don't ever let your lives become so full that you
don't have time to slow down and listen. First, find time to carefully
listen to the Lord. Hear his heart for you and the direction that He has
for you. Your days can be filled with so much more meaning when you
stop to heed God's direction. The whispers of the Holy Spirit are there,
daily nudging at our hearts, but we miss them in the busyness of life.
Please slow down, listen to that still small whisper, and you will find
that you don't waste near as much time as you heed the guidance of
the Lord.

Also, slow down and listen to those around you. Sometimes we miss sharing the love of Christ because we haven't slowed down to hear how people are truly doing. The common question, "How are you?" gets answered quickly and dismissed. My children, if you will only slow down to hear that answer, you may find yourself in tune to someone who is hurting, a heart that is aching, an opportunity to pray, and a time to be available for the Lord. Please practice the art of active listening. You will be given more opportunities in life as you stop to listen and respond in loving ways.

And whatever you do, please do your best not to interrupt someone when they are speaking. Being an active listener means hearing someone out from the first word that leaves their mouth to the last word. You have no idea where they are going with their thought, so be careful not to interrupt. I promise as you sit to listen intentionally and carefully, you will hear everything you need to know for sharing your next thought.

> *My son, pay attention to what I say; listen closely to my words. Do not let them out of your sight, keep them within your heart; for they are life to those who find them and health to a man's whole body.* (Proverbs 4:20–22)

DEAR FATHER GOD, please help me to slow down and tune into what Your Spirit is whispering to my heart. May I not be so busy that I miss the moments you have for me simply because I wasn't listening. Lord, I pray that my ears will be attentive to those who are hurting. May I engage in conversation with a heart that's ready to respond in love and ears that are open to hear what's truly on someone's heart.

"We should listen with the ears of God that we may speak the Word of God."   — Dietrich Bonhoeffer

Day 24

WALK TALL AND STAND STRONG

Be on guard; stand firm in your faith [in God, respecting His precepts and keeping your doctrine sound]. *Act like* [mature] *men and be courageous; be strong.*
— 1 Corinthians 16:13 (AMP)

One of the greatest lessons I want you to learn is to activate your faith instead of your fear. The enemy wants to keep you in a place of fear, minimizing what you can do in God, but God has given you the ability to move forward in faith even when something doesn't make sense.

David pursued a giant with only a slingshot in hand and defeated his enemy. Joshua and the Israelites faced an indestructible wall around the city of Jericho. They moved forward in faith, claiming what God had promised them. Daniel faced a den of lions on his knees. Prayer was his weapon of choice, and God kept the lions' mouths shut.

Many men and women around the world are facing unbelievable things with a faith in God that cannot be shaken. They face the giants of this world, the walls of persecution, and the lions of destruction. Yet they do not give up. They do not waver in their faith, and they stand their ground.

My prayer is that you will walk by faith and not by sight. May you not fear the days to come but may you stand strong in all that God has for you. You will have a choice every day to activate you faith or your fear. As you place your eyes on Jesus, the Author and Perfector of your faith, you can walk tall and stand strong. Remember, absolutely nothing is impossible with God. There is nothing you will face in life that is bigger or stronger than the One who is in you.

Little children, you are from God and have overcome them,
for he who is in you is greater than he who is in the world.
(1 John 4:4, ESV)

DEAR FATHER GOD, please teach me what it means to walk tall and stand strong. May I face every day with anticipation for all that You can and will do. May my heart not fear the plans of my enemy but may I move forward in what You have for me. I choose to live by faith, not by sight. I will feed my faith and not my fear. In You, I move forward today. Thank You, Lord!

"Faith sees the invisible, believes the unbelievable, and receives the impossible.   — Corrie ten Boom

Day 25

THERE IS ALWAYS ROOM FOR GROWTH

The wise will hear and increase their learning, and the person of understanding will acquire wise counsel and the skill [to steer his course wisely and lead others to the truth].
— Proverbs 1:5 (AMP)

Life Lesson: Never Stop Learning

One of the greatest things that you can do in life is to find a way to learn something new every day. You will never know everything. You will never have life all figured out. Sure, there will be times when you think you know it all. But I promise you that you don't. I promise that everywhere you go in life and everyone you meet is a new opportunity to learn and grow in Christ. My prayer is that you never stop being a student.

I encourage you to ask a lot of questions from those who are wise in the areas of life that God has entrusted them with. You will find many people along life's journey who are experts in their fields because they have taken the time to study extensively. Stop and learn from them. Sit under wise counsel and listen as they share amazing words of wisdom. Glean from as many people as possible so that you can grow in your own walk with the Lord.

Test everything that someone says against God's Word. God's Word is the authority on life, and anything you learn from anyone should be able to stand the test. If it's not backed up by God's Word, then I encourage you to let it go. May your mind only be filled with things that honor God, and may you find room to grow every day that you live. I pray that even if you make it to the ripe old age of a hundred, you are still learning. I pray that you get excited every time you sit down to read the Bible. Look for something new and embrace what God wants to teach you every day.

Life will be so full of adventure, joy, and pleasant experiences if you take the time to learn along the way. Growth is a daily, weekly, monthly, and yearly thing. It does not happen overnight. In fact, often you will not see your growth from day to day. It will be when you look back at a year or years of your life that you see growth. That growth comes from your daily choice to learn and glean from those around you.

> ***Take hold of instruction; [actively seek it, grip it firmly and]*** *do* ***not let go. Guard her, for she is your life.*** (Proverbs 4:13, AMP)

DEAR FATHER GOD, may I never stop being a student of Your Word. I pray that I will seek You with all of my heart and mind. Lord, I pray that as I walk through life, I will look for opportunities to grow. May I never fear what I don't know but may I always embrace the opportunity to learn something new. I pray that I will daily grow in all that You desire me to be and all that I can be in You!

"The stiff and wooden quality about our religious lives is a result of our lack of holy desire. Complacency is a deadly foe of all spiritual growth. Acute desire must be present or there will be no manifestation of Christ to His people."

— A. W. Tozer

Day 26

OBEDIENCE IS THE KEY

Be careful to listen to all these words which I am commanding you, so that it may be well with you and with your children after you forever, because you will be doing what is good and right in the sight of the LORD your God.

— Deuteronomy 12:28 (AMP)

> ### Life Lesson: Obey God's Word

*Y*ou will find there is a great temptation to disobey God's Word on a daily basis. This temptation can be fierce, and it can lead you in a direction that will ultimately destroy your life. Your life can be saved from the pangs of death if you daily surrender yourself to God's direction and His ways. Proverbs 14:12 says, "There is a way that seems right to a man, but in the end it leads to death." If you decide to feed your flesh in what you think is right, ultimately you will pay the cost.

The enemy we fight desires that this be the direction you go in. He wants nothing more than to steal, kill, and destroy you (John 10:10). It's God who has a plan for your life. Find that plan by seeking Him in His Word. And when you are faced with the temptation to disobey, remind yourself what the cost is. The cost is far greater than you should be willing to pay.

Daily, even minute by minute, sometimes you will be given an opportunity to obey God. You will have many moments throughout your day where you can honor God by your thoughts, your words, and your actions. Remember to take each thought captive as every thought you have becomes a word or action if you do not make it obedient to Christ (2 Corinthians 10:5). Test these thoughts and see if they honor the Philippians 4:8 principle. If they do not honor this—and I mean in every attribute of this verse—then pluck the thought out. Those thoughts are not your friend; they will lead you away from God's best for you! May you find that obedience begins in your mind, and you daily have the choice to honor God with every thought you think!

> *But this thing I did command them: "Listen to and obey My voice, and I will be your God, and you shall be My people; and you will walk in all the way which I command you, so that it may be well with you."*   (Jeremiah 7:23, AMP)

DEAR FATHER GOD, please help me to recognize when my thoughts are not honoring to You. I pray that I will take each thought captive and make it obedient to Christ. May I tune in to You and obey Your voice. I want to walk in Your ways and follow You with all my heart. Please daily discipline me to be obedient to You and choose the path of life!

"Radical obedience to Christ is not easy…It's not comfort, not health, not wealth, and not prosperity in this world. Radical obedience to Christ risks losing all these things. But in the end, such risk finds its reward in Christ. And he is more than enough for us."

— David Platt

Day 27

KEEP IN STEP WITH THE LORD

But I say, walk habitually in the [Holy] *Spirit* [seek Him and be responsive to His guidance], *and then you will certainly not carry out the desire of the sinful nature* [which responds impulsively without regard for God and His precepts].

— Galatians 5:16 (AMP)

> ### Life Lesson: Walk in the Spirit

There will be little things that happen in your day all along life's journey. Pay attention to these little moments. The moments when you feel something in your heart toward someone, when you are moved to compassion, and when you feel that maybe you just shouldn't follow through on something quite yet. Tune in to what the Holy Spirit is doing in your life. Never move forward without peace because God promises a peace that passes all understanding that can and will guard your heart and mind in Christ Jesus (Philippians 4:7). Only move forward when you feel that peace.

As you walk throughout your day, open your eyes to the smallest of things. Notice the little things and respond to them. God can use you in ways that you can't begin to imagine if your eyes are open. Walk through your day available for Him so that He can use you wherever you go. There are people hurting all around you, many of whom have yet to experience eternal security in Christ. If your eyes are open, your heart is ready, and your mouth is prepared to give an answer, you can be the one to share Jesus with them.

Walking in the Spirit and keeping in step with the Lord is the most exciting adventure that life can hold. God has great things in store for you and will take you places you can only dream of. The more you learn to be available for Him and seek His kingdom purpose, the more you will experience the adventure of a lifetime that awaits you in Him.

> *Those who live according to the sinful nature have their minds set on what that nature desires; but those who live in accordance with the Spirit have their minds set on what the Spirit desires. The mind of sinful man is death, but the mind controlled by the Spirit is life and peace.*
>
> (Romans 8:5–6)

DEAR FATHER GOD, please give me an undivided heart. I pray that my feet will go where You lead me, that my heart will respond to those who are hurting, that my mouth may be prepared to give an answer for the hope that is within me, and that my hands will always be available to serve You. Lord, there is no greater adventure than following You and going where You lead. Please use me to make a difference today and please give me an increased sensitivity to the leading of Your Holy Spirit in my life.

> " 'Wait on the Lord' is a constant refrain in the Psalms, and it is a necessary word, for God often keeps us waiting. He is not in such a hurry as we are, and it is not his way to give more light on the future than we need for action in the present, or to guide us more than one step at a time. When in doubt, do nothing, but continue to wait on God. When action is needed, light will come."
>
> — J. I. Packer

Day 28

ONLY SPEAK WHAT EDIFIES

Do not let any unwholesome talk come out of your mouths, but only what is helpful for building others up according to their needs, that it may benefit those who listen.

— Ephesians 4:29

Life Lesson: Speak Truth and Life

The truth behind this verse in Ephesians continues to amaze me. We are to not let any unwholesome talk come out of our mouths. Unwholesome talk can come in the form of a lie, slander, gossip, foul language, critical and judgmental words. Our words have the power to bring life or death to any situation. We can speak words that edify the body of Christ and lift it up or words that destroy the body. It's always our choice!

I want to teach you the importance of choosing your words wisely. Remember, "when words are many, sin is not absent but he who holds his tongue is wise" (Proverbs 10:19). The longer your tongue is moving and the more your mouth is open, the more susceptible you are to saying something that doesn't please the Lord. In James 3, we learn that the tongue is an unruly muscle and cannot be tamed by any man. It's in spending time with Jesus and recognizing what doesn't please Him that we can teach ourselves to speak only what edifies the body.

This will be a lifelong challenge, a daily discipline, and you will need to constantly keep your mind on the things of Christ so that out of the overflow of your heart, your mouth speaks what is pleasing to the Lord. I know it will be tough. I battle it every day, but I know there is no battle worthier than this one. Your words can change the atmosphere of a room. You can bring people to life with what you say. The choice will always be yours, my children, and I pray you choose wisely with every word you say.

> ***When there are many words, transgression and offense are unavoidable, but he who controls his lips and keeps thoughtful silence is wise.*** (Proverbs 10:19, AMP)

DEAR FATHER GOD, please help me keep a tighter reign on my tongue. May I speak only what edifies the body of Christ and brings You glory. Lord, I pray that I will be more like Your Son, Jesus, and choose words that bring life to others. Please help me to recognize when my words do not honor You and daily remember to surrender my tongue to You!

"The Christian faith is meant to be lived moment by moment. It isn't some broad, general outline–it's a long walk with a real Person. Details count: passing thoughts, small sacrifices, a few encouraging words, little acts of kindness, brief victories over nagging sins."

— Joni Earekson Tada

Day 29

REMEMBER WHO YOU ARE

Yet to all who received him, to those who believed in his name, he gave the right to become children of God— children born not of natural descent, nor of human decision or a husband's will, but born of God.

— John 1:12–13

Life Lesson: Keep Your Identity in Christ

My children, this world is going to bombard you with its ideas of how to live life, and it will try to get you to identify with all that it offers. But I want you to remember who you are. In a world that is constantly changing, I want you to remember the One who never changes. In the busyness of the day, I want you to know that God is never too busy for you. When life hands you challenges and you lose sight of who you are, God will be there. Cast your cares, your burdens, your life struggles on Him because he cares for you. He will always be enough for you!

I pray that you never let a job, a relationship, a degree, an accomplishment, your looks, or your talents become your identity. I pray that you will find your identity in Christ alone. My hope is that you will always remember what Jesus did for you on the cross. May you never lose sight of this but may you constantly be aware that God sent his one and only Son for you. Jesus died for you. He died so that you can spend eternity with God. May that never stop amazing you!

And as you go through your days, may you find security in Christ alone. You will find that insecurity plagues everyone. The enemy is constantly at work trying to blind people from their true identity. When we walk in this blindness, we serve the god of this world; but when our eyes are open, we serve our Heavenly Father. Live with eyes wide open and serve with a heart abandoned to God and His purpose. Never lose sight of who you are and whose you are. In Christ, you are a new creation. You are no longer identified by your sin, your past, your struggles, or anything else in this life. You are a child of God, bought by the precious blood of Jesus. You are more valuable than you can imagine, and God will blow your mind with His plans for you if you let Him.

> *The Spirit Himself testifies and confirms together with our spirit [assuring us] that we [believers] are children of God. And if [we are His] children, [then we are His] heirs also: heirs of God and fellow heirs with Christ [sharing His spiritual blessing and inheritance], if indeed we share in His suffering so that we may also share in His glory.* (Romans 8:16–17, AMP)

DEAR FATHER GOD, please help me to daily find my identity in Christ. May I not waver back and forth with this world and the mold they want to try to fit me in. May I be free from the expectations of this world and free to serve Christ with all of my heart. I am a child of God, loved by my Abba Father, and created to do good works in Christ Jesus. Lord, please help me to never lose sight of who I am in Christ Jesus.

"Define yourself radically as one beloved by God. This is the true self. Every other identity is illusion."

— Brennan Manning

Day 30

APPRECIATE THE GIFT GIVER

Therefore go and make disciples of all nations, baptizing them in the name of the Father and of the Son and of the Holy Spirit, and teaching them to obey everything I have commanded you. And surely I am with you always, to the very end of the age.

— Matthew 28:19–20

Life Lesson: Intentionally Share Jesus

The best way you can show appreciation for the gift of salvation that you have been given is to give it to others. God freely gave it to you, and now He has entrusted you to share it with those you come in contact with. You don't have to cross an ocean to share Jesus. You don't have to be gifted in evangelism or even a great teacher. You, my child, have everything you need to share Jesus in your personal testimony. God has given you a testimony that testifies of His goodness in your life, and now He wants you to use it.

When you go through life, whether it be school or work or shopping or any number of things, make it your intention to share Jesus wherever you go. In fact, the Great Commission actually breaks down in the Greek to say, "As you go…" You don't share Jesus when you feel like it. You don't make him a prize that you show off. He is your life. He is everything that you are about. Jesus is the center of your very existence, and without Him, your life has no purpose.

As you go through life doing the normal things that we do, I pray that you will be available to share Jesus wherever you go. May your actions speak of a love you have known in God, and may your heart be ready to share an answer with those who seek the hope that you have in Christ. I pray that you will never be ashamed but live your life fully abandoned and fully aware of God's purpose for you. May sharing Jesus be so natural for you that you could do it in your sleep. I pray this will be your life's ambition. May you seek to share Jesus with as many people as you can while living on this earth. And may there be a trail behind you that doesn't end when you enter into eternity.

That's what counts in eternity. Nothing here will matter. No amount of money, no amount of fame, and no amount of recognition will last. Only the things you do for eternity will truly matter. I pray you always keep eternity in focus and live a life that matters! May you always **MAKE YOUR MOMENTS COUNT**!

> *But in your hearts set apart Christ as Lord. Always be prepared to give an answer to everyone who asks you to give the reason for the hope that you have. But do this with gentleness and respect.*
>
> (1 Peter 3:15)

DEAR FATHER GOD, I pray that I will live my life ready to share who Jesus is. May I never shy away from an opportunity to talk about the hope that I have in Christ. Please give me the strength to daily prepare my heart and mind for the conversations that will come, and may I never underestimate the power of the testimony You have given me. Thank you, Lord!

"The Great Commission is not an option to be considered; it is a command to be obeyed."

— Hudson Taylor

Maximize Your Moments

Always Show Grace

Listen Carefully

Activate Faith, Not Fear

Never Stop Learning

Obey God's Word

Walk in the Spirit

Speak Truth and Life

Keep Your Identity in Christ

Intentionally Share Jesus

BIBLIOGRAPHY

AZ Quotes. "Veronique Vienne." Accessed February 15, 2016. http://www. azquotes.com/quote/1271326.

Barba, Effie Darlene. *Ultimate Inspiration—God's Plan of Love*. Bloomington, Indiana: Author House, 2012

Barton, Ruth Haley. *Strengthening the Soul of Your Leadership: Seeking God in the Crucible of Ministry*. Westmont, Illinois: Intervarsity Press, 2008. Kindle edition.

Bavinck, Herman. *Our Reasonable Faith*. Grand Rapids, MI: W.B. Eerdmans Pub., 1956.

Blackaby, Henry T., Claude V. King, and Richard Blackaby. *Experiencing God: Knowing and Doing the Will of God*, Revised and Expanded. Nashville: LifeWay Press, 2007.

Bonhoeffer, Dietrich, and John W. Doberstein. *Life Together: The Classic Exploration of Christian Community*. New York: Harper & Row, 1954.

Brainy Quote. Accessed January 11, 2016. http://www.brainyquote.com/search_ results.html?q=thomas edison.

Chan, Francis. *Crazy Love: Overwhelmed by a Relentless God*. Colorado Springs: David C. Cook, 2008.

Christian Quotes. "223 Quotes About Grace." Accessed March 21, 2016. http://www. christianquotes.info/quotes-by-topic/quotes-about-grace/.

Corrie Ten Boom Quotes. "Corrie Ten Boom Quotes." Accessed March 13, 2016. http://l.facebook.com/l/ TAQG4penPAQGQmKgXlwc2pDqugZug3KiT06hP9PmgG4n5_g/www. goodreads.com/author/quotes/102203.Corrie_ten_Boom.

Crosswalk. "40 Powerful Quotes from Corrie Ten Boom." Accessed March 21, 2016. http://www.crosswalk.com/faith/women/40-powerful-quotes-from-corrie-ten-boom.html.

Elliot, Elisabeth. *Keep a Quiet Heart*. Ann Arbor, MI: Vine Books, 1995.

Engage. "Slogans That Awakened the Church: Option or Command?" Accessed March 21, 2016. http://engagemagazine.com/content/slogans-awakened-church-option-or-command.

Fox, Jennifer, Christopher Markus, Steve McFeely, Michael Petroni, and C. S. Lewis. *The Chronicles of Narnia: The Voyage of the Dawn Treader*. New York, NY: Harper, 2010.

Lemmel, Helen H. "Turn Your Eyes Upon Jesus." Recorded 1922.

Manning, Brennan. *Abba's Child: The Cry of the Heart for Intimate Belonging*. Colorado Springs, CO: NavPress, 2002.

Neal, Nicola. *Journey into Love: The Unfailing Power That Restores Lives*. Shippensburg, PA: Destiny Image Publishers, 2014.

Newton, John. *Cardiphonia: Or, The Utterance of the Heart in the Course of Real Correspondence*. Edinburgh: Balfour and Clarke, 1819.

Packer, J. I. *Knowing God*. Downers Grove, IL: InterVarsity Press, 1973.

Picture Quotes. "PictureQuotes.com." Accessed February 12, 2016. http://www.picturequotes.com/be-who-you-are-not-who-the-world-wants-you-to-be-quote-9397.

Platt, David. *Radical: Taking Back Your Faith from the American Dream*. Colorado Springs, CO: Multnomah Books, 2010.

Quotes Daddy. "Related Quotes." Accessed February 18, 2016. https://www.quotesdaddy.com/quote/1392203/thomas-j-powell/each-person-creates-the-life-they-live-by-choosing.

Sandra Butler. "MLK Quote of the Week: Faith Is Taking the First Step…" The King Center. Accessed February 24, 2016. http://www.thekingcenter.org/blog/mlk-quote-week-faith-taking-first-step.

Sproul, R. C. *Essential Truths of the Christian Faith*. Wheaton, IL: Tyndale House, 1992.

Spurgeon, C. H. *Spurgeon's Sermon Notes: Over 250 Sermons including Notes, Commentary and Illustrations*. Peabody, MD: Hendrickson Publishers, 1997.

Tada, Joni Eareckson. *Glorious Intruder: God's Presence in Life's Chaos*. Portland, OR: Multnomah, 1989.

Tolkien, J. R. R. *The Lord of the Rings: The Fellowship of the Ring*. London: HarperCollins, 2001.

Tozer, A. W., and Samuel Marinus Zwemer. *The Pursuit of God*. Harrisburg, PA: Christian Publications, 1948.

Voskamp, Ann. *One Thousand Gifts: A Dare to Live Fully Right Where You Are*. Grand Rapids, MI: Zondervan, 2010.

Wiersbe, Warren. "A Compilation of Christian Quotes and Popular Bible Verses." Accessed February 03, 2016. ChristianQuotes.info.